A Good Man in Evil Times

The story of Aristides de Sousa Mendes –
the unknown hero who saved countless
lives in World War II

JOSÉ–ALAIN FRALON

Translated by Peter Graham

VIKING

VIKING

Published by the Penguin Group

Penguin Books Ltd, 27 Wrights Lane, London W8 5TZ, England

Penguin Putnam Inc., 375 Hudson Street, New York, New York 10014, USA

Penguin Books Australia Ltd, Ringwood, Victoria, Australia

Penguin Books Canada Ltd, 10 Alcorn Avenue, Toronto, Ontario, Canada M4V 3B2

Penguin Books (NZ) Ltd, Private Bag 102902, NSMC, Auckland, New Zealand

Penguin Books Ltd, Registered Offices: Harmondsworth, Middlesex, England

First published in France by Mollat as *Le Juste de Bordeaux* 1998
This translation first published in Great Britain by Viking 2000

1 3 5 7 9 10 8 6 4 2

Set in 11.5/15pt Monotype Bembo
Typeset by Rowland Phototypesetting Ltd,
Bury St Edmunds, Suffolk
Printed in Great Britain by Clays Ltd, St Ives plc

A CIP catalogue record for this book is available from the British Library

ISBN 0-670-88803-6

Contents

List of Illustrations

All the photographs belong to António de Moncada de Sousa Mendes unless otherwise indicated.

Acknowledgements

It would not have been possible to write this book without the help of Aristides de Sousa Mendes's children, in particular Pedro Nuno de Sousa Mendes and Marie-Rose Faure, or without the cordial assistance of António de Moncada de Sousa Mendes, who has so proudly kept alive the memory of his grandfather.

The enthusiasm of Brother Jacques Rivière in Bordeaux was an inspiration. Diana Andringa in Lisbon was kind enough to allow me to draw on the considerable work she did for her television documentary, *O Cônsul Injustiçado* (*The Proscribed Consul*).

I would like, then, to extend my warmest thanks to all those mentioned above, as well as to everyone else who, from Brussels to San Francisco, kindly provided me with direct or indirect information about the life of Aristides de Sousa Mendes.

José-Alain Fralon

Prologue

Bordeaux 1940. They waited, in their thousands, in the sweltering summer heat. Some had left Paris the previous day. Others, who had come from as far away as Riga, Warsaw and Berlin, had spent several weeks, if not months, on the road to exile. They were all fleeing the barbarians whose shadow now darkened the whole of Europe.

They were called refugees. We now know that a death sentence hung over them. To save their lives, all they needed was a signature on their passports. But the only man who could sign their passports did not have the right to do so – because they were Jews, Poles, or stateless persons, when they were not of 'undefined nationality' or simply undesirable.

We can be sure that many people in a position to do something about their plight would have shirked their responsibilities and obeyed their superiors' orders, on the grounds that it had nothing to do with them.

But one man did not. His name was Aristides de Sousa Mendes.

1. The Twins of Beira Alta

Our story begins in the nineteenth century. In the small hours of the morning of 19 July 1885, Aristides de Sousa Mendes do Amaral e Abranches was born at his parents' home, Casa do Aido, in the village of Cabanas de Viriato in northern Portugal. His twin brother, César, had come into the world about an hour earlier, and was registered as having been born late on 18 July. The die was cast: César, the serious, obedient and introverted 'elder' brother, would always look after Aristides, his outgoing, generous and impulsive 'little' brother.

The twins spent their childhood in Beira Alta, a small northern province which is traversed by Portugal's highest mountain range, the Serra da Estrêla, some of whose peaks rise to an altitude of 2,000 metres. 'It is one of the heartlands of Portugal,' the Portuguese novelist and journalist Fernando Dacosta[1] tells me. 'Its inhabitants possess the quintessential traits of the Portuguese: sensitivity, love of the land, a fondness for authority, and a sense of honour.'

Cabanas de Viriato lies in the centre of a triangle formed by three unusual towns: Viseu to the west, Guarda to the east, and Coimbra to the south. 'Haughty Viseu, the former capital of Beira Alta, lives off the produce of the surrounding countryside and is convinced it is the birthplace of Viriatus, the Lusitanian hero who so frightened the Romans,' writes Hélène Gourby in *Le Portugal*.[2]

Guarda is Portugal's highest town. Reputedly 'ugly and cold', it is indeed a rather forbidding and dour fortress, which once kept watch over the border with Portugal's hereditary enemy, Spain, a country described in another Portuguese saying as the source of 'neither good wind nor good marriage'.

To the south is the light-filled Coimbra, whose university dominates the upper part of the town. Recaptured from the Saracens at the beginning of the eleventh century, it was the capital of a county which, according to Jean-François Labourdette's *Histoire du Portugal*,[3] constituted the second political core of the future Portugal, the first being the formation of a county farther to the south, which was dominated by the Mendes dynasty.

Coimbra was the capital of the kingdom in the twelfth century and the starting point of the *Reconquista*, which gave birth to Portugal as we know it, a country that can justifiably claim to have the oldest frontiers in Europe.

It was in Coimbra, too, that one of the strangest and most beautiful love stories of all time took place: Pedro, son of

King Afonso IV, fell in love with Inês, the lady-in-waiting of his wife, Constança de Castela. The king, wishing to estrange the beautiful Inês, had her locked up in the convent of Santa Clara in Coimbra. There she wept so much that her tears gave birth to a fountain of love.

When Constança died in 1345, Pedro joined Inês in the convent and married her secretly. Ten years later, the king arranged for her to be murdered. Pedro rebelled, seized the throne, revealed his marriage and had the hearts of his wife's murderers torn out. Her corpse was exhumed and the members of the court filed past her in a sublime and morbid tribute. This true story is related by Luís de Camões in *The Lusiads*. It also inspired Henri de Montherlant's play *La Reine morte*.

The mountainous north, where Sousa Mendes's family came from, was much more influenced by the church than the south of the country. Its peasant families were tied down to tiny plots of land owned by local patriarchs, unlike the migrant farming proletariat of the south. It would be only a slight over-simplification to say that Portugal divides into a conservative Catholic north and a progressive atheist south.

Portugal, as we have seen, has the oldest frontiers on the European continent; history has given it a true homogeneity; and it is one of the few European countries to have an almost perfect linguistic unity. Yet it is indisputably divided into two worlds – *o Mediterrâneo* and *o Atlântico* – 'which are different in every way except for their awareness of belonging to the same nation', as Jacques Marcadé puts it in his book *Le Portugal au XXe siècle*.[4] In addition to this north–south divide between the two banks of the Tagus, *Aquém* and *Além Tejo*, which was created by geographical factors, there are differences between the Portugal of the coast and the Portugal of the hinterland, which were created by history.

Aristides and César de Sousa Mendes came from the landowning, Catholic, conservative and monarchist northern aristocracy. Their father, José, was an appeal court judge in Coimbra. According to one of Aristides's grandchildren, 'José de Sousa Mendes was a very just and thoroughly good man, who cared a great deal about the fate of prisoners and turned down all the gifts – of oil, oranges, wine and chickens – that his neighbours kept on offering him.' A family photograph of 1900 shows him to be a powerfully built man sporting a black suit and a gold watch chain, who has a good head of dark bushy hair, and equally dark eyes that seem to sparkle like embers.

His wife, Angelina, had the reputation of being extremely strict. For example, when one of her women servants told her she intended to get married, Angelina retorted: 'If you marry, you won't work here any more.' The servant did not get married.

On 28 April 1889, less than four years after the birth of César and Aristides, a certain António de Oliveira Salazar was born in Vimieiro, some twenty kilometres from Cabanas de Viriato. His family was of modest means and deeply

Catholic. They lived in a single-storey house that gave directly on to the street. António's father was the manager of a landowner's estate.

'The future master of Portugal,' the French journalist Paul-Jean Franceschini wrote after Salazar's death in 1970,[5] 'must have been affected by the fact that during his childhood he admired and loved his devout father, and heard him each evening settling the accounts and calculating the harvest of the farm he managed.' Salazar's mother, an extremely pious woman, left such a mark on him that, contrary to Portuguese custom, the young António took her name: Maria do Resgate Salazar.

One naturally wonders whether the young Salazar ever met Aristides or César de Sousa Mendes. He probably did, but from a distance, like any poor young kid who watches the children of the rich go by, with a mixture of resentment and admiration. After all, his father could well have been the manager of the Sousa Mendes estates. The Sousa Mendes family, one of the best known in the region, was closely associated with the history of Portugal. Aristides's grandfather, Manuel Alves de Sousa, was a wealthy landowner. He was descended from the private secretary of King João VI, who left his country and took refuge in Brazil when he thought Napoleon's armies were about to invade Portugal.

Aristides's grandmother, Raquel Augusta Mendes da Gama, whose family possessed a palatial home, was also of rural aristocratic stock.

Aristides's father, José, married the strict Angelina do Amaral e Abranches, a descendant through her mother, Maria dos Prazeres Ribeiro de Abranches, of Viscount de Midões, who came from one of Portugal's oldest and noblest families. Viscount de Midões went to prison during the civil war at the beginning of the nineteenth century because he had defended 'liberal' ideas. He was one of those who countered the champions of royal absolutism by calling for a charter to be drawn up.

In connection with the Abranches family, legend has it that a Portuguese knight by the name of Álvaro Vaz de Almada travelled to England at the end of the fourteenth century in order to defend the honour of a lady who had been insulted by 'Teutonic' soldiers. He later displayed such courage during the conquest of the town of Avranches in Normandy that he received the Order of the Garter and the title Earl of Avranches. Portuguese pronunciation turned Avranches into Abranches. The two sons of Aristides de Sousa Mendes who as United States citizens took part in the Normandy landings of June 1944 consequently found themselves, so to speak, on home ground.

Finally, to conclude this brief portrait of the family, mention needs to be made of Francisco Ribeiro de Abranches, Aristides's uncle on his mother's side, who was 'the king's preacher' – or *pregador régio* – at Alcobaça, one of Portugal's largest monasteries. He was apparently a man of such eloquence that his sermons brought tears to the eyes of the hundreds of people who would come to listen to them. That did not, however, stop him leading a double life: he was married and had a string of children.

Aristides, César and a third brother, José Paulo, who was born in 1895, grew up in the family home at Aveiro and went to school in Mangualde.

A family photograph, taken in the garden at Cabanas de Viriato at the turn of the century, gives a strange impression. It could be the result of that particularly Portuguese combination of sadness and nostalgia, *saudade*, which gives the *fados* their flavour, or, more prosaically, of an oversight on the photographer's part. But no one is smiling at the camera. The young José Paulo, who has long hair and is wearing girl's clothes as was customary at the time, is flanked by the imposing figure of his father, José, and his mother, Angelina, who is wearing a long black skirt and a white embroidered bodice. As for the twins, who are dressed in elegant light-grey suits, they too seem to have an infinitely melancholy expression on their faces. Perhaps they are already thinking of going out and conquering the world.

The two brothers entered Coimbra University, Portugal's only such establishment until a faculty opened in Lisbon in 1911. Housed in the former royal palace, it was regarded as one of the centres of European culture, on a par with Bologna, Paris, Oxford or Cambridge. It was then the largest and oldest university in the Iberian peninsula after Salamanca University.

From the Porta Férrea (Iron Gate) to the Paços das Escolas (Palace of the Schools), the décor is majestic. The same is true of the Sala dos Capelos (Hall of Hats), which is decorated with seventeenth-century *azulejos*, and which is reached by crossing Via Latina, so called because it used to be forbidden to speak any language other than Latin there. Overlooking the hall, which is lined with the portraits of Portuguese sovereigns, is a gallery reserved for women. Needless to say, at that time Coimbra University was attended only by men; women were admitted only in the 1940s.

Important occasions determined the rhythm of student life, rather as at Louvain University, of which Aristides became so fond thirty years later. Students were dressed in fringed black gowns and wore ribbons of different colours, depending on their faculty. The ribbons were burnt in May in the course of the year's most celebrated festival. Aristides and César graduated in law, which was the most prestigious degree, in 1907. Their grades show that for once Aristides had proved himself a better student than César.

Salazar entered Coimbra University the year the twins went down. Like all children from a humble background in the deeply religious Portugal of the time, he was educated at a seminary. His parents wanted him to take holy orders. He was a devout and studious pupil who won a string of prizes in various subjects, but never lost his enthusiasm for theology and, more particularly, St Thomas Aquinas.

In 1908 Salazar gave up the idea of joining the priesthood because he had no deep-felt vocation, but he remained strongly attached to the church throughout his life. He once resigned as a minister and brought down a government for the simple reason that it was considering restricting church processions and bell-ringing.

At Coimbra, Salazar was in the same 'republic' (dormitory) as the future Cardinal Manuel Cerejeira, with whom he would later share power – political power in Salazar's case, and spiritual in Cerejeira's. Cerejeira's path would also cross that of Aristides de Sousa Mendes, though scarcely to the cardinal's credit, as we shall see.

When the '*vermelhos*' ('Reds') burst into the theology faculty at Coimbra in 1910, Salazar protested against the damage caused by their strong-arm tactics. That incident left him with a lasting aversion to crowds. 'Where there is order, do not let in disorder' was one of the aphorisms that later featured in an anthology of his thoughts.

After taking his doctorate, Salazar became a professor of political economy. He always inculcated into his pupils a doctrine based on the principles his father followed when doing the estate's accounts: never spend a penny more than you earn.

Aristides, César and Salazar were born in a country which, although experiencing a period of apparent political stability towards the end of the nineteenth century, had been through a terrible ordeal. At the beginning of the nineteenth century, Portugal was ruined by three Napoleonic invasions. The French, when conquering the country, and the English, when defending it, 'lived off it and plundered it systematically, as well as behaving like vandals and stealing works of art', according to Labourdette.[6] There was considerable loss of human life, with a death toll possibly as high as 100,000.

The Napoleonic invasions also explain why the Portuguese showed so little enthusiasm for the 'liberal' ideas that the invaders brought with them. 'From then on,' Labourdette goes on, 'liberalism was tarred with the antipatriotic brush in Portugal, while patriotism long seemed indistinguishable from traditionalism, a fact that greatly hindered any political evolution.'[7]

Another consequence of the Napoleonic invasions was that Brazil severed its connections with Portugal. When the royal court was set up in Rio de Janeiro so as to escape the imperial armies, a mortal blow was dealt to the colonial system: it accustomed Brazil to governing itself. It gained independence in 1822. As for Portugal's economic dependence on the British, it intensified to a point where by the beginning of the twentieth century 70 per cent of all Portuguese exports were going to Britain.

'During the nineteenth century Portugal, like Spain, was dragged down by social and economic archaisms and fell further behind the rest of Europe,' Labourdette concludes.[8]

César and Aristides de Sousa Mendes, like their fellow

scion of Beira Alta, António de Oliveira Salazar, could scarcely have guessed then that they would be directly caught up in the tragic turmoil of twentieth-century Europe.

2. The Carefree Happiness
of a Large Family

A photograph dating from early 1910 shows César and Aristides de Sousa Mendes do Amaral e Abranches in their brand-new ceremonial diplomatic dress. Their moustaches are twirled, their jackets brocaded with gold, their sabres sheathed at their sides, their cocked hats firmly perched on their heads and their hands protected by white gloves. They cut a fine figure as they walk into the Holy of Holies, the Palácio das Necessidades, the seat of the Portuguese Foreign Ministry.

Perched on one of the hills overlooking Lisbon, this delicate-pink baroque palace contains hundreds of rooms that give off a pleasant whiff of wax polish and leather-bound books. It was the favourite residence of Carlos I and Amélia of Orléans, Portugal's last queen. It was in that hushed atmosphere that diplomats were initiated into the foreign policy of a country that had dominated the world and still intended to maintain its rank.

Given that their father was a judge and they were law

graduates, Aristides and César would clearly have embarked on a career in the legal profession had it not been for their irrepressible wanderlust – a malady that is impossible to cure in certain individuals who feel the call of the sea, especially if they are Bretons or Portuguese, strange peoples that feel at home only in their native village or in some remote part of the world.

So the twins opted for a career in the foreign service. César, restoring the natural order of things and getting his revenge for what he had experienced when graduating from Coimbra University, got a better grade than Aristides in the competitive examination that they had to take at the beginning of their career as diplomats. Subsequent events proved that César was indisputably a more orthodox, if not a more effective, diplomat than his younger twin.

On 12 April 1910 Aristides arrived in Demerara, in British Guiana, where he had been appointed second-class consul. A few months later, on 5 October, the republic was proclaimed in Lisbon, ushering in a period of political turmoil. One can only speculate as to how Aristides, in his remote posting, reacted to the news from Portugal – news that the government had legalized divorce, recognized the right to strike and expelled religious communities from state-owned property. He doubtless took a poor view of it all. The Sousa Mendes clan had always respected the natural order of things – a united family, workers that work, and a church in the middle of each village.

As he began his career, Aristides embarked on another task, that of starting a family. In 1909 he married Angelina, a woman three years his junior who was to play a crucial role in his life. She was his first cousin, being the daughter of António de Sousa Mendes, the brother of Aristides's father José, and of Clotilde do Amaral e Abranches. Aristides and Angelina's first child, Aristides, was born that same year in Coimbra.

Many other children followed, as the Sousa Mendes moved from one diplomatic posting to another. At Passal, the 'palace' in Cabanas de Viriato where the family met for the holidays, the flags of the countries where their various children were born were proudly displayed half-way up the main staircase.

The first document in Aristides de Sousa Mendes's file at the Foreign Ministry is a request that he should be allowed to return to Lisbon for health reasons. His request was accepted, and on 1 April 1911 he returned to the Portuguese capital. After spending a few months in Galicia, he left on 10 November to take up his second posting, in Zanzibar. He arrived a week later. In those days, diplomats and their families travelled by boat. It was an important posting, as the sultanate of Zanzibar was a neighbour of Mozambique, then a Portuguese colony.

The Sousa Mendes's second child, Manuel, was born in 1912 in Portugal. According to Professor Veríssimo Serrão,[1] Aristides de Sousa Mendes took advantage of a trip to British

East Africa to visit the large Portuguese colony in the Kenyan capital, Nairobi. He also met compatriots in Mombasa.

José, Clotilde and Isabel were all born in Zanzibar, in 1912, 1913 and 1915 respectively. Aristides spent the period from 17 March 1914 to 17 June 1915 in Lisbon, while his family remained at Cabanas de Viriato. They then all returned to Zanzibar. The political situation in Portugal was becoming increasingly tense. The first attempt by certain groups to set up a strong-arm regime came to nothing. But it was only a matter of time before they succeeded.

The Great War encouraged the formation of a highly illusory united front. On 9 March 1916 Germany declared war on Portugal, on the grounds that Lisbon had acceded to a British request that it should confiscate any of the Central Powers' vessels that sought refuge in its ports. Portugal sent an expeditionary force to Flanders and launched several expeditions in Angola and Mozambique. But the Portuguese army, then in the process of being reorganized, was ill-equipped to fight against much more modern armies.

'The Portuguese gave a brilliant account of themselves on the battlefields of Flanders, but to no avail,' Jacques Marcadé writes.[2] 'Because there was little to show for their valour, a feeling of resentment sprang up in the army at a time when the regime, which was dangerously weak, depended increasingly on its armed forces. That was something which one of the officers in the expeditionary corps, Colonel Gomes da Costa, who later became a general, was to remember.'

Unrest among the population was mounting. There was an increasing number of hunger riots, like the celebrated Revolução da Batata (the potato revolution) of May 1917. As more and more lists of the dead and wounded in action in Flanders and Mozambique were published, the Portuguese found it increasingly difficult to understand the reasons for the conflict, or why they were fighting a war for the first time in more than a century. Later, Salazar skilfully exploited his people's 'neutralist' aspirations.

The World War had indirect repercussions on Zanzibar, a British protectorate then in dispute with the German colony of Tanganyika (Tanganyika and Zanzibar united in 1964 to form Tanzania). Diplomats familiar with the region approved of the policy adopted by Sousa Mendes, who was decorated by the Sultan of Zanzibar with the Second-Class Medal of the Shining Star, the highest distinction that could be awarded to a foreigner. Another token of the Sultan's esteem was his gift of a magnificent sultan's ceremonial dress. Looking at the wonderful photograph of Sousa Mendes carrying a curved scimitar and a dagger inlaid with silver, one can imagine the laughter, or tears, that he must have prompted in his five small children.

In 1917 there was another addition to the family, Geraldo, whose godfather was none other than the Sultan. The following year, on 13 May, the Sousa Mendes family moved again, this time to the cities of Curitiba and Porto Alegre in southern Brazil. They stayed in Brazil a little more than a year. Their third daughter, Joana, was born there in 1918.

They could have stayed there longer if Sousa Mendes, in August 1919, had not been temporarily suspended by the Foreign Ministry, which regarded him as hostile to the republican regime. The Catholic, conservative and monarchist Sousa Mendes was undoubtedly no republican at heart. Here again there is a parallel with the experience of Salazar, who was also sanctioned in 1919 on suspicion of having taken part in a royalist plot.

Sousa Mendes responded to his ministry's decision in two stages. First, as an act of defiance, he emphasized his aristocratic origins by officially requesting that he should from then on be known as Aristides de Sousa Mendes do Amaral e Abranches, and not just Sousa Mendes. Once he had done that, he wrote to his superiors on 22 May 1920, explaining that he had financial problems and had been 'forced to take out a loan in order to provide for his family's needs'.

Following the birth of Pedro Nuno in 1920 in Coimbra, Aristides and Angelina now had eight children. Given that the Sousa Mendes family took their servants with them wherever they went, even to the other side of the globe, and that Passal, their house in Cabanas de Viriato, was becoming increasingly well appointed, it is easy to see that Aristides had difficulty in making ends meet without a regular salary.

This was neither the first nor the last time that Aristides

had money problems. He was someone who always spent without counting the cost and believed that the mere idea of balancing one's budget showed a lack of breeding. A very different man from the thrifty Salazar, Aristides was destined to spend much of his life 'juggling' with financial problems. It is certain that César came to his rescue more than once. His more cautious elder twin had not been suspended, even though he had exactly the same political opinions as Aristides. César, whose career took him to many countries, was comfortably affluent; but his house in Mangualde was in no way comparable to Aristides's palatial home.

Aristides was reinstated in 1920 and posted to San Francisco, where his ninth child, Carlos, was born that same year. The consul ran into some problems with certain associations of Portuguese residents in that city, because he had stood up for his poorest compatriots when they protested against the working conditions to which they were subjected by their employers, who were also Portuguese, but much better off.

Sebastião was born in 1923, the year when Salazar first entered the political arena by agreeing to stand as a parliamentary candidate on a 'Catholic centrist' list. He was elected, attended one parliamentary sitting, and resigned that same evening. All he said by way of explanation was: 'Parliament terrifies me.'

In 1924 the Sousa Mendes family of twelve, still accompanied by the same servants, returned to Brazil. Teresinha was born in Porto Alegre in 1925. The family returned to

Lisbon in 1926, before moving to Vigo, the Spanish town closest to Cabanas de Viriato. Sousa Mendes was in Spain on 28 May 1926, when General Gomes da Costa and General Oscar Carmona incited their regiments to rise up against the republic. The insurrectional committee in Coimbra offered Salazar the Finance Ministry. He remained a minister for five days.

In an interview with the daily *Progreso*, which was published in Vigo, Sousa Mendes said that 'the military dictatorship had been greeted with delight' in Portugal. In January 1928, the poet Fernando Pessoa, who was born in 1888, also came out in support of the new regime in *O Interregno*: 'There are no options other than a military dictatorship that can ensure the country's salvation and renaissance.'

Although the pronunciamento took a farcical turn when one of the putschists, Gomes da Costa, was ousted by the other, Carmona, an authoritarian regime was set up. Two attempted left-wing uprisings were crushed. When he was elected President of the Republic in April 1928, Carmona gave Salazar the job of Finance Minister. In his first speech, Salazar was at least frank: 'I know very well what I want and where I'm going. [. . .] When the time comes for me to give orders, I shall expect [the country] to obey me.' By imposing new taxes and making drastic cuts in public spending, he kept his pledge to rebalance the budget.

That 'time' soon came: on 5 June 1932, António de Oliveira Salazar became prime minister. Did he want power?

Did he appropriate it? Or was he merely content to be given it, against his will, in Portugal's interest? The fact remains that he was now in power – and would remain so for a long time to come.

In his first government, Salazar appointed César de Sousa Mendes to the post of Foreign Minister. César had already had a distinguished career, in the course of which he had experienced fewer ups and downs than his brother. In 1916, he was appointed chargé d'affaires in Tokyo. When Hirohito was made emperor in 1926, César enjoyed the signal honour, in his capacity as the most senior member of the diplomatic corps, of being received at the imperial palace and photographed in the emperor's company. Next to César in the photograph is his wife, Maria Luísa. César's great-nephew, António, was later told by a woman friend of his great-aunt that she was 'the most beautiful woman in the diplomatic corps in Tokyo'.

To understand the osmosis and mutual affection that united the vast Sousa Mendes family, one needs to keep in mind the very large number of marriages that took place between cousins. Thus, three of Aristides's children married three of César's children. After the death of his first wife, César himself married Maria da Assunção, the daughter of an extremely wealthy marquess who was descended from a director of the Royal Mail, and who owned a vast palace in Lisbon. Maria's brother, the Marquess of Penafiel, was to die while serving in the ranks of the Portuguese legion that later

came to General Francisco Franco's aid during the Spanish
Civil War. He wore a white uniform and had refused to
wear a helmet.

César was ambassador to Sweden when Salazar recalled
him to Lisbon in 1932. In the meantime, Aristides had been
posted to Belgium in 1929, taking with him yet another
child, Luís Filipe, who had been born in Spain in 1928. He
had hoped to land a really important posting, such as China
or Japan, but had to make do with the Consulate General in
Antwerp. It probably turned out to be what was best for him
and his family.

All the evidence that can be gleaned from photographs
and letters of the time suggests that despite some personal
tragedies the Sousa Mendes family was extremely happy in
Belgium, a haven of freedom. More than thirty years later,
when António, Aristides's grandson, deserted so as to avoid
having to serve in Salazar's army, he quite naturally took
refuge in that country.

It is worth taking a closer look at the various members of
the Sousa Mendes family at this point in their lives, when
they were reunited for the last time before being parted by
the vicissitudes of the war that would engulf Europe.

When, for example, the family arrived in Brussels early in
1929, 'We all sat in a circle on the pavement round a tiny
square waiting for our father to settle a few problems,'
remembers Pedro Nuno, the eldest of the surviving children.
The Sousa Mendes moved into a boarding house in the

Brussels suburb of Ixelles with their twelve children and their servants. Aptly enough, it was called 'Chez Nous'.

The Sousa Mendes then moved to Louvain, a town which, although in Flanders, has a Catholic university (the oldest in the country) where lectures are given in French. The atmosphere in that university town, which was at once studious and lively, serious and schoolboyish, must have reminded Aristides of Coimbra. It was in Louvain that João Paulo was born in 1932.

Another moment in the lives of the Sousa Mendes family can be brought back to life, thanks to some personal memories and a couple of photographs taken in their large garden in Louvain in 1932. It was probably a Sunday, since the elder sons are wearing suits and ties. The occasion might have been the birthday of one or other of the children – an ideal opportunity to take some family snaps.

First, it was the turn of the boys, all nine of them. The four 'big' ones, wearing dark suits and white shirts, stand behind their younger brothers.

– Aristides, the eldest, is twenty-three and has neatly swept-back hair. Of a serious and sombre disposition, he smiles little and is not thought to take after his father. His health is not good: he suffers from asthma. He is happiest when playing the piano or sitting before his drawing-board. He has just begun reading law at Louvain University.

– Manuel, twenty-one, is also at Louvain University. A charming and brilliant student, he would come first in the final competitive exams at the faculty of political science, to his father's delight.

– José, twenty, also greatly admires Manuel, his idol. Although his glasses give him a serious air, he never managed to settle down in life. He would take refuge in piano playing.

– Geraldo, fifteen, who is flashing a broad smile and has slightly dishevelled hair, is the jolliest and funniest member of the family. And above all the most talkative. He is said to have inherited from his grandfather, a judge, or from his ancestor, a preacher, a gift for carrying conviction. 'Everyone would listen to him when he spoke,' say all those who remember him today.

– Pedro Nuno, twelve, is wearing a Belgian scout's uniform and carrying a bush hat in his hand. What he adores above all is drawing. It was he who, at his father's request, later designed the car-cum-coach which Aristides had custom-built so he could drive his whole family around.

– Carlos is less than a year younger than Pedro Nuno (he was also born in 1920). A rather uncommunicative, shy, secretive and bookish lad, he was nicknamed 'the archbishop' by his brothers and sisters. Already an accomplished pianist, he began his schooling in Louvain and completed it in Portugal.

– Sebastião, nine, was nicknamed 'the American' by the rest of the family. Was it because he was born in San Francisco, or because he was the only fair-haired child in the family? He is a determined and enterprising child who is never at a loss for an idea.

– Luís Filipe, four, is a bright child who went to primary school in Louvain.

– João Paulo, who is not yet one year old, is the 'Belgian' member of the brood, since he was born in Louvain.

Then it was the girls' turn to pose for the photographer. There are four of them, but as there were always friends or cousins at the Sousa Mendes home, eight young ladies stand arm in arm looking at the camera with a mixture of effrontery and shyness.

– Clotilde, nineteen, is about to complete her law studies – quite an achievement, as it was not all that common for women to go to university at that time. As the eldest daughter, she also plays the role of second mother. She loves oil painting and the piano. As we have already seen, music formed an integral part of family life. 'The beautiful' Clotilde got married to her first cousin, Silvério, at Cabanas de Viriato in 1940. They had eleven children.

– Isabel, seventeen, found a husband before her elder sister: in 1937, she married Jules d'Aout, a Belgian student who was reading commercial science at Louvain University. It was said that Aristides had great difficulty in saying goodbye to Isabel, a sunny, fun-loving girl who was adored by her brothers and sisters. 'Anyone who tries to steal my girl had better watch out!' he would joke.

– Joana, fourteen, had 'rather an explosive' temperament,

her younger brother Pedro Nuno remembers. If she did not get her own way, she was capable of 'smashing the place up'.

– Teresinha, seven, differed from everyone else in the family in that she had no penchant for school, and even less for the piano.

It would be an understatement to say that Aristides loved his children. He passed on to them his extraordinary energy, love of life and cultural curiosity. Every Wednesday, a well-known painter would come and give the children lessons. But it was music that cemented the household together more than anything else. Several piano and violin teachers came to give the children lessons. Aristides, who loved opera, was the family's leading singer and conductor.

His home in Louvain was visited by several illustrious figures, including the playwright Maurice Maeterlinck and Alfonso XIII, the Spanish king who had abdicated in 1931. And it was there that Aristides's younger brother, the naval commander José Paulo, who loved mathematics, discussed relativity with a certain Albert Einstein.

Aristides was very proud of his children and loved taking them to official receptions. Pedro Nuno remembers a particularly 'starchy' meal at the Quai d'Orsay (the French Foreign Ministry): 'Almost all of us were there at table with our father. At the beginning of the meal, he gave us the usual advice: "Now you must behave and not talk too loudly." At the very moment when he asked us to be careful with our glasses and not to knock anything over, the sommelier brought a bottle of wine to the table. My father, who was very expansive and talked with his hands, suddenly swivelled round and knocked the bottle over with his elbow, spilling its contents on to the white tablecloth. We spent the whole meal giggling, and no one more than my father.'

Aristides would also sometimes ask his elder children to replace him or his wife at official functions. In 1934, it was Clotilde who accompanied him when he attended the 'Joyous Entry' – a ceremony during which new Belgian sovereigns present themselves to a city and are paid its respects – of King Léopold and Queen Astrid into Antwerp. As Aristides was the doyen of the diplomatic corps, Clotilde offered a spray of flowers to the beautiful Astrid, whose accidental death a few months later left the whole of Europe numb with grief. When the ceremony was over, a protocol officer at the Belgian court made a point of introducing Aristides to the king, in the belief that they did not know each other. Léopold smiled as he shook Aristides warmly by the hand, and said: 'Ah, my good friend the Portuguese ambassador!'

'On another occasion, my father rushed home and said: "I can't go to a concert this evening," ' Pedro Nuno remembers. ' "The governor of the province is going to be there. You must go in my place and pay your respects to the governor and tell him something has prevented me from coming." '

So Pedro Nuno, who was not yet seventeen, had to put

on a dinner jacket and go along to the concert to hear Verdi's *Rigoletto*. Little did he realize that a few months later he would also be dragooned into going to a concert by a Hungarian violinist. 'Luckily, I loved music,' he remembers. 'And anyway my father wanted me to become a diplomat, so he was training me for my future job.'

On one occasion when Aristides was invited to a ball with his wife, who hated social occasions and only really felt happy at home, he asked Pedro Nuno to go in his place with his two sisters, Clotilde and Isabel. 'We spent the whole night dancing to swing music and wolfing the buffet to the astonishment of the governor and his suite,' Pedro Nuno remembers.

Aristides's enormous complicity with his children went hand in hand with a very great respect. Every evening, before going to bed, his children would go and say goodnight to their father, whom they addressed with the formal *você*, and kissed his hand.

Aristides de Sousa Mendes's financial situation improved, notably thanks to the dues the consulate was allowed to charge boats putting into Antwerp that had come from or were bound for Portugal. Yet he still did not budget in a manner that would have pleased the rigorous Salazar. In 1932, he justified a further request for an increase in his mission expenses by sending his ministry a cutting from a Belgian newspaper which gave statistics showing how the cost of living had risen.

The Sousa Mendes family felt so at home in Belgium that the eldest children – Aristides, José, Clotilde, Isabel, Geraldo, Joana and Pedro Nuno – wrote to the Portuguese president asking him to allow their father to stay in Louvain so they could continue their studies there. Aristides was told in reply that he should not mix up the affairs of state with family affairs.

One summer, when the Sousa Mendes family was returning to Cabanas de Viriato by train, a Spanish border policeman at Irún who, typically enough, was a stickler for principles, failed to understand why a family of diplomats was travelling third class. He tried to get them to change compartments. His behaviour both delighted and irritated Aristides, who replied that he was entitled to travel as he saw fit.

Probably because he was tired of travelling by train, Aristides asked Pedro Nuno to think about designing a 'car' that would enable them all to travel together. The boy got down to work and pored over his drawing-board. He gave the design to his father, who showed it to the Ford garage in Antwerp. The result was a weird prototype, half car and half coach, of which only one example was manufactured. A beautiful cream colour, it could accommodate the whole family. The children called the contraption the Expresso dos Montes Hermínios, after a mountain in Beira Alta.

The arrival of the Sousa Mendes family in Cabanas de Viriato, usually for the holidays, was understandably always something of an event. Those servants who had stayed behind busily prepared the house, or 'the palace', as it was known locally. The village would be seething with expectancy.

'As soon as we saw "the coach" arrive, we children would rush forward, and the festivities would start,' remembers Barros Martins, who was a sacristan at the church of Cabanas de Viriato. It is easy to understand why the children were overjoyed. No sooner did Aristides get out of the vehicle than he would rummage in his suitcases, fish out a huge bag of sweets and throw handfuls of them to the kids. 'He also threw us chocolate coins,' Barros Martins remembers. 'And even when there were no chocolates left, the golden or silver paper they were wrapped in was something we really treasured.'

Then the family could enter 'the palace'. The building, properly known as Quinta de São Cristóvão, or St Cristobal's Farm, which Angelina de Sousa Mendes had inherited, is situated at a spot called Passal. It was dominated by a statue of Christ the King several metres high which 'Aristides do Passal', as he was known locally, had had made in Louvain.

A workman remembers the labour involved in going to fetch the statue, which was in three pieces, at the station, loading it on to a lorry, taking it to Cabanas de Viriato and erecting it on its pedestal with the help of ropes. César must have known what a huge sum the whole operation cost, since Aristides called on him once again to help finance it.

At the base of the statue of Christ the King, whose very

gentle countenance seemed to protect both the house and
the rest of the village, there was an inscription:

> Lord God, our father
> And our all-powerful King,
> Bless Cabanas
> And its people.

If he had had the time and money, Aristides would have
liked to have built a flight of steps running up from 'the
palace' to the foot of the statue.

'The palace' was originally no more than a fine, imposing
bourgeois building, like César's at Mangualde, a village some
thirty kilometres away. But Aristides dreamt of better things,
and built not only an additional storey but a whole new
wing, next to the servants' quarters.

That gave the mansion a much grander look. Facing the
front door inside the building was a wooden staircase that
divided into two flights half-way up. On the landing, a
showcase contained all the flags of the countries where Aristides had been posted and where his children had been born.
The family's coat of arms – Abranches's two eagles and two
swords, Castelo-Branco's lion, Figueiredo's fig leaves and
Evreux's five pinions – could be seen not only on the ceiling
but on the chairs that surrounded the huge table in one of
the dining-rooms.

The dining-room was never capacious enough. Not only

did Aristides have a large family, but it was his custom to invite to lunch or dinner all those who happened to be at Passal at mealtimes. That meant there were twenty to thirty people at table virtually every day.

The rest of the house was equally luxurious: there were several fine libraries, a chapel, three drawing-rooms, including a Chinese one, two Bechstein pianos and a pianola, six bathrooms and more than ten bedrooms. Each of its windows afforded a fine view over Beira Alta.

The house's vast grounds were surrounded by a wall. On the far side of this 'garden', members of the family needed simply to cross a road – today Rua Aristides de Sousa Mendes – to reach São Cristóvão church. In the adjoining graveyard some ten mausolea bearing the names of the region's grand families surrounded the Sousa Mendes family's mausoleum, complete with its coat of arms.

On the other side of the house was the village school. At times when he did not happen to be posted anywhere – between Porto Alegre and Zanzibar, or San Francisco and Antwerp, some of the Sousa Mendes children attended the school for a few months. One of those was Luís Filipe, who asked the teacher: 'I would like you to tell me the history of Portugal, sir.'

On the first day after their arrival, Aristides and Angelina would go round the village paying their respects to local notables. 'In fact they constantly stopped to say a few kind words to everyone they met,' says Barros Martins, 'and asked them for their news.' They went to mass in the village church every morning at 7 a.m. 'When they came out,' Martins says, 'they would call me over and say: "Come here Zezito" – that was my nickname – "go and see Maria in our kitchen and she'll give you some breakfast."'

Aristides, who cut an elegant figure even if he was in shirt-sleeves, always wore his black hat – 'the consul's hat', as it was known in the village. For important receptions he put on his ceremonial uniform, to the great admiration of the villagers.

Thursday was 'the day of the poor'. All those who did not have enough to eat were given a plate of soup or some beans and bread. Even when the Sousa Mendes were abroad, José Augusto, their manager, was given instructions to leave the door of the main kitchen open to anyone who wanted to come in to eat or simply keep warm. 'Aristides was often there in the kitchen, standing in front of the big ovens in which the bread was baked,' Martins remembers. 'I can still see him, looking so sad at the sight of all the needy, especially children who were barefoot.'

Aristides loved playing and laughing with the village children. 'He'd always ask my cousin to imitate a policeman's whistle,' says a villager. 'It was a treat to watch him – he was so smiling and cheerful.' 'He never lost his temper, despite all the responsibilities he had,' says another. 'In the evening we could hear music coming out of Passal. There were lots of receptions and people laughing. We'd go as close as we could to see what was going on.'

As for Angelina, 'a saint', she spent a lot of time outside the house with her daughters and servants. 'She and her daughters were so unaffected that we couldn't distinguish between employers and servants,' a Cabanas woman says.

The Sousa Mendes household had its fair share of grief as well as of happiness. In 1933 Raquel was born in Louvain. She died of an unknown disease eighteen months later, causing immense grief among the whole family. To cap everything, Manuel died on 4 April 1934 as a result of a burst blood vessel. The death of the elegant Manuel, possibly the most gifted of the Sousa Mendes sons, particularly traumatized José, who never got over the death of the elder brother he so admired.

In 1934 the bodies of Manuel and Raquel were placed in the family vault at Cabanas de Viriato. Their coffins, which had been sent from Louvain, left Passal with a cortège of mourners, who walked to the church with Geraldo playing Chopin's *Funeral March* on the violin. There were similar scenes of grief when a faithful servant, Ana Borges, was buried.

Joy, on the other hand, was the keynote of Clotilde's wedding in 1940. It was attended by the whole family. 'There were so many flowers that the newly-weds walked on a carpet of petals,' the older villagers remember.

The petals were soon to turn into thorns. The first to suffer was César. His ministerial career, which had begun in 1932 when he joined Salazar's first government, lasted a little less than a year. When he expressed the opinion that disciplinary proceedings should be taken out against a Portuguese diplomat posted abroad, he had crossed swords with Salazar's small circle of close friends, which varied in composition depending on circumstances.

He then clashed with Salazar himself during a cabinet meeting at which higher education was discussed. César, who had been ambassador to Sweden, was struck by the importance that country attributed to education, and said so. The dictator bluntly contradicted him, arguing that it would be a mistake to change things or develop education too much. Deeply affected by the death of his eldest son, who was also his private secretary, César lost heart. One day he got a telephone call from Salazar, who said: 'I would like to thank you for your services, minister.' César was taken aback and asked the secretary general of the ministry what that sibylline remark could have meant. 'He was simply letting you know that you were no longer a minister.'

César left to take up the post of Portuguese ambassador in Warsaw. There, he received a letter from Aristides – the two brothers often corresponded – in which he said what he thought of Salazar: 'A plague on him, and may his name be uttered with contempt if he should ever become the cause of our collective disgrace!'

Meanwhile Salazar strengthened his grip on power. In 1933, in the preface he wrote to a series of interviews he gave António Ferro,[3] he described himself in the third person as follows:

He is a man who belongs to the government but did not want to govern. He attended one session as a member of parliament and never returned to the house. He was a minister; he stayed five days in the job, left and did not want to return. [. . .] He has not conspired or given orders to any group. He has not intrigued. He has overcome no adversary by organized or revolutionary force [. . .].

It seems to be immaterial to him whether he stays or leaves, and yet he stays. [. . .] But the problem and the uncertainty remain at the same level. How does a man who has not been a conspicuous candidate for government, who has not sacrificed all the energies of his being to that end, who has not proclaimed himself capable of leading, commanding, executing or getting executed a government programme, whether his own or not, and who regards power more as a duty of conscience than as a right that he might enjoy through the force of conquest, summon up the willpower necessary not to be stopped halfway to his goal unless it comes from an ambition to command?

True, it is well written. The moral dilemma is well explained. His self-questioning is admirable. And yet the same man who in 1933 said he did not like power enjoyed undivided rule until 1968. To put his reign in a French context, it could be said that he saw out the Third Republic, the Popular Front, the Vichyist French State, the Liberation, the Fourth Republic, de Gaulle's return to government, and the Fifth Republic.

'Salazar, who wanted to be a schoolmaster and had the best interests of his pupils – the Portuguese – at heart without ever asking them for their opinion on the matter, was quite simply a dictator. His only great good fortune was to have been compared with men like Hitler, Franco and Mussolini, who were much more effective in their line of business than he was,' says a Portuguese teacher.

Fascist movements were beginning to loom ominously over Europe. It is true that Salazar did not go in for Mussolini-like sabre-rattling or Hitler's 'pagan' extremes. As for Franco, who helped him come to power, he found his notions of foreign relations very limited and attempted to give him advice. It was said that Salazar was the Caudillo's 'foreign minister'.

Although Salazarism has been described as a form of 'fascism without a fascist movement', one should not overlook the Portuguese Mocidade, an ideological and paramilitary youth training organization, which Mário Soares, the future president of the Portuguese republic, describes in the following striking terms:

We were forced to join it from the age of ten. Our uniform – a skullcap, a green shirt, khaki trousers and boots – was compulsory. Our belts had a big metal buckle which sported the letter S. Later on, the government claimed that the S referred not to Salazar, but to 'Serving one's country'. When we stood to attention, we had to give the fascist salute, with our arm outstretched. The chief in charge of each parade would yell a first question: 'Portuguese, who lives?' We then had to shout as loudly as we could: 'Portugal, Portugal, Portugal!' Then he asked us even more loudly: 'Portuguese, who commands?' We had to reply: 'Salazar, Salazar, Salazar!'[4]

The repressive machine swung into action. In March 1934, Salazar caused a bloodbath when he put down the workers' uprising at Marinha Grande. In 1935, Fernando Pessoa, quoted by Antoine de Gaudemar in his preface to Pessoa's *Lisbonne*,[5] showed that he had understood the true nature of the regime very early on. In a long unpublished text, which he wrote directly in French for the review *Colóquio*,[6] he painted a portrait of a 'hypocritical' Salazar who was 'harsh and sly', 'the product of a concentration of narrow-mindedness', 'who hates dreamers because they dream'.

Pessoa's chief target was censorship: 'I have to publish an article only when I agree with the government's action, and say nothing if the opposite is true. [. . .] The obvious solution is to publish nothing . . . to make a vast literature of silence.'

Following a big anti-Communist demonstration in 1936, Salazar created an armed militia called the Portuguese Legion, and set up a formidable political police service. In September of that year, after a rebellion by the crews of two warships who wanted to join the Spanish Republicans, the government forced all government employees to take an anti-Communist oath.

In the interest of those whose 'minds have been torn by this century's doubt and negativism', Salazar announced, 'we have tried to restore the comfort of the great certainties of life. We have not discussed God or virtue; we have not discussed our fatherland or its history; we have not discussed authority or its prestige; we have not discussed the family or its morals; we have not discussed work or the glory of working.'

Aristides watched events unfold from Louvain. He was now apparently better disposed towards Salazar. In a letter to César on 26 January 1935, after asking his brother for a further loan to help pay for the statue of Christ the King, which had already arrived in Cabanas de Viriato, he reported a conversation he had had with Salazar during his last stay in Lisbon. 'We talked for an hour,' Aristides wrote. 'He was amiable and cordial. I got the feeling that even if he wants to know things, he has no power of decision. He is very frightened and has no intention of allowing himself to become the victim of a murder attempt. May God protect him.'

On 16 June 1937, on the occasion of a 'festival of the Portuguese Race', whose ostensible purpose was to commemorate the great poet Luís de Camões, Aristides de Sousa Mendes gave a lecture in which he launched into a ringing tribute to the Portuguese race and to Lusitanian heroism in general, and proclaimed himself to be 'a legionary of the nationalist Holy Crusade'.

He again ran into financial problems. On top of that, he was subject to disciplinary proceedings because he had been late in transferring funds to the ministry. In 1938 he asked for the job of second-class head of delegation in China or Japan. He got neither.

The government appointed him consul in Bordeaux. Aristides de Sousa Mendes was about to perform the role that fate had allotted him.

3. Why Does a Man Start Disobeying?

Even though the international situation was steadily deteriorating, Aristides de Sousa Mendes declared shortly before leaving for Bordeaux: 'The war won't take place. Commonsense will prevail.' His wife, Angelina, who may have been a more intuitive person, was much more pessimistic and had sombre forebodings.

They arrived officially in Bordeaux on 29 September 1938, accompanied by some of their children. Aristides soon gave fresh proof of his generosity: when several Portuguese cyclists who had taken part in a race told him they did not have enough money for their return fare, he paid for their hotel rooms, food and train tickets out of his own pocket.

The Sousa Mendes installed themselves at 14 Quai Louis-XVIII, a street along the embankment named after the king most loved by the inhabitants of Bordeaux, because he lifted a British blockade. Built on the site of a former chapel, their 350-square-metre apartment overlooked the Garonne river, which was flowing sluggishly at that time of year.

The Quai Louis-XVIII is located right in the heart of the city. It runs along one side of the huge, 12.6-hectare Esplanade des Quinconces, with its imposing monument to the Girondins, and leads to the Chartrons quarter, one of the most important centres of the world wine trade, and the city's port, which was then still a hive of activity, with its toing and froing of boats from all over the world. The family settled into the fourteen rooms of the apartment, two of which were used as the consulate's offices.

The consular secretary, José Seabra, welcomed Sousa Mendes. Born in Lisbon on 17 November 1906, he had arrived in France in 1930 and worked at the consulate since May 1936. A small bespectacled man, he was discreet and respectful of authority. Polite to the point of preciosity, he was regarded by some as 'affected'.

'He didn't talk much,' Pedro Nuno remembers. 'I think he had been greatly affected by the death of a Bordeaux woman, with whom he was deeply in love – every Saturday he would place a bunch of flowers on her grave.' Seabra was soon won over by Sousa Mendes's generosity, drive and enthusiasm.

The Sousa Mendes's loyal servant, Fernanda Dias de Jesus da Silva, had also travelled to Bordeaux. Born in Carregal do Sal, and a pupil of Salazar's sister at primary school, she had accompanied the Sousa Mendes family to Antwerp. 'Working for a diplomat was more important to me than going to college,' she told Carlos Magno, a journalist on

Expresso who interviewed her in 1996.[1] Her mother had entrusted her to Sousa Mendes because she was sure that her future would be assured.

In Bordeaux, the '*petiza*' ('little girl'), as the whole family called her, worked as a factotum: 'I was a concierge, I looked after the children, I answered the telephone, and I lent a hand whenever it was necessary.' According to Magno, 'she had such a faraway look that almost sixty years after the event she seemed still to be on the embankment of the Garonne'.

In 1938 Andrée Cibial, who as a teenager had sworn she 'would one day marry a consul', entered Aristides de Sousa Mendes's life. Cibial was born in Limoges on 6 February 1908. Her father was a furniture delivery man in Bordeaux who very soon abandoned his family; her mother died in 1911 when Andrée was only three. She was brought up by her aunt on her father's side and her husband, who lived in the small Dordogne town of Ribérac. After attending high school in nearby Bergerac, she studied at the Bordeaux conservatoire, where she passed her *agrégation* (the highest competitive examination for teachers) in music and got a *proxime accessit* for singing.

She was a cheerful, elegant and cultured woman who sang wonderfully. She was one of those rather zany people who possess not a trace of self-doubt, and who are capable of expending a vast amount of energy to achieve their aims, however far-fetched and unlikely they might seem. After all, she had told friends she would marry a consul – not just a diplomat, but a consul.

She met an African diplomat in Bordeaux. But they did not get on. However, as soon as she set eyes on the smart, charming and naturally aristocratic Aristides, she was fascinated to a degree she had not imagined possible. He, too, was attracted by Andrée, whose freedom and disregard for the proprieties set her at opposite poles from Angelina, his loyal, devoted and devout wife.

Andrée was one of those people who seem to have no family or country. Her relationship with Aristides was not straightforward. Pedro Nuno remembers how one evening his father asked him to go to the cinema with 'a lady' – who turned out to be none other than Andrée.

The situation in Lisbon was getting more and more difficult. Miguel Torga describes the winter of 1939–40 as follows: 'The political atmosphere, which had become suffocating, smothered any attempt at independent action and discouraged even the most determined. The Catholic-cum-military dictatorship, which was embodied in the will of a single man, had turned the nation into a continuum of terror, where the censor's stamp guaranteed silence, and where those who refused to resign themselves to the situation stifled in the lurking and nightmarish presence of the secret police.'[2]

The members of the Sousa Mendes family soon got back into their routine, filling the apartment on Quai Louis-XVIII

with their customary music-making and *joie de vivre*. But that
was not to last.

Angelina had been right: on 1 September 1939, as a curtain-
raiser to one of the most appalling tragedies in the history of
the world, German troops invaded Poland.

Salazar opted for neutrality, even if, towards the end of
the war, he allowed the Allies to use Portugal's base in the
Azores. 'His wobbly balancing act is still admired by some,'
notes a former Lisbon journalist, 'but they forget perhaps
that in certain situations, when the alternative is abomination,
the mere fact of not choosing already boils down to a choice.'

Salazar's supporters argued that in view of German plans
to invade the Iberian peninsula it was vital not to 'upset'
Hitler. Churchill and Montgomery soon saw the limitations
of Salazar's double game and eventually came to hate the
Portuguese dictator.

When he launched his slogan, 'co-operative neutrality',
Salazar knew perfectly well that it was little more than a
smokescreen. 'Jurists will have a tough job explaining it,' he
quipped. He himself had a tough job justifying his silence
when first the Allies, then the Japanese, had no compunction
in violating Portugal's neutrality by invading Timor, then a
Portuguese possession.

Aristides and Angelina decided to take their children back
to the safety of Cabanas de Viriato. It was to be a difficult
trip. As Aristides had not asked his superiors for permission

to leave his post, he wanted to get the journey over with as quickly as possible and pushed the Expresso dos Montes Hermínios as hard as it would go. Fernanda, the '*petiza*', sat on the front seat between Aristides and Angelina. They had to stop several times so she could get out and be sick.

'We were terribly hungry,' she remembers. 'We had no provisions, and no money either, so we ate berries we found by the roadside.' The 'minibus', with its diplomatic number plates and its anxious occupants, did not go unnoticed on the Spanish roads. It was closely followed by another car, that of a Belgian princess who was fleeing France.

Near Salamanca, Aristides missed a bend and overturned on the edge of a ravine. He immediately extricated himself from the vehicle and, realizing that no one had been hurt, shouted: 'Thank heavens! Thank heavens! Thank heavens!' Fernanda passed out for a few seconds. She was more frightened than hurt. But the vehicle had to remain by the roadside for a whole day before it could be righted and continue on its way.

By a curious but unwelcome coincidence, General Franco's wife drove past the Sousa Mendes family. Seeing his diplomatic number plates, she stopped and asked if she could be of service to him. At the Spanish–Portuguese border, Aristides decided not to enter Portugal in case news of his escapade somehow reached Lisbon. So he entrusted his minibus and his whole family except Angelina to one of his cousins, who drove them on to Cabanas.

Little did Aristides know that he had just crossed a watershed in his life. He was now back in his huge Bordeaux apartment, alone with Angelina. On 13 November 1939, he received – like every other Portuguese diplomat abroad – a circular from the Foreign Ministry which radically called into question Portugal's centuries-old tradition of hospitality and officially introduced a hitherto unknown element of racial or religious segregation into the question of immigration.

Circular 14, as it came to be known, began with a convoluted preamble about 'the abnormal current circumstances' and the need 'to adopt measures, if only temporarily', to 'prevent abuse', 'without however wishing to make entry into Portugal too difficult for foreigners in transit travelling to Lisbon in order to leave for America, whom we do not wish to hinder'. The circular then forbade consuls to grant passports or visas to the following categories of people without first referring the matter to the Foreign Ministry:

– Aliens of undefined, contested or contentious nationality, stateless persons, Russians, and holders of 'Nansen passports' (named after a Norwegian diplomat who had arranged for refugees and displaced or stateless persons to be given identity papers by the Society of Nations, the ancestor of the United Nations).

– Aliens who in the consul's opinion were unable to provide valid reasons for entering Portugal or whose passports contained indications suggesting they would be unable to return freely to their countries of origin. (Consuls were also expected to make investigations in the case of all aliens with a view to establishing whether they had any means of support.)

– Jews expelled from their countries and stripped of their nationality.

That was too much for Aristides de Sousa Mendes: he rebelled. Yet a mystery remains: how was it that a man of nearly fifty-five, who had had fourteen children, who had never opposed the Portuguese government (except when it was republican), who had serious financial problems, and who could think only of completing his stint in Bordeaux and securing a more prestigious posting in a more far-off land, came to disobey authority when his whole upbringing had taught him to obey?

He committed his first act of resistance before he had even received Circular 14. On 27 November and again on 6 December 1939, he asked Lisbon for permission to grant visas to an Austrian national, Arnold Wiznitzer, and his family. In other words, he was following the instructions of Circular 14 – except that he had already granted the visas.

On 2 February 1940, Eduardo Neira Laporte, a professor from Barcelona who had fled the Franco regime, went to Quai Louis-XVIII and explained his problem to Sousa Mendes: he wanted to go to Bolivia, a country which was prepared to take him in with his family. In order to do so, he needed to take a Lisbon-bound boat at La Rochelle, and then sail on to Nicaragua. Sousa Mendes immediately applied to Lisbon for an authorization, but got no reply.

A month later, the professor came back in a state of great agitation: if he did not take the Lisbon boat next day, he would miss his connection for Latin America. On 1 March, Sousa Mendes signed the visa without waiting for a reply from Lisbon. When it came, on 11 March, it was negative. On 12 March, Laporte and his family put in at Lisbon with visas dated 1 March. They were regarded as undesirable but allowed to embark for Bolivia. The secretary general of the Foreign Ministry, Count Tovar (whose path we shall cross again later on), sent a sharp reprimand to the consul in Bordeaux.

In a letter that Aristides sent César in May 1940, he complained: 'The ministry is giving me a lot of trouble. [. . .] The man [Dr Laporte] and his family would never have been able to leave here if I hadn't done that [given them a visa]. In the end, everything went through quite normally, but the Portuguese Stalin decided to pounce on me like a wild beast. I hope that will be the end of the matter, but I can't rule out another attack. I've no problems with my conscience.'

That was not the end of the matter as far as Aristides was concerned: he was to give the 'Portuguese Stalin' further cause for complaint on many other occasions. On 30 May 1940 he issued a Portuguese passport and transit visa for Spain to a couple from Luxembourg, who were fleeing the Germans.

The woman, aged thirty-five, was Portuguese, *née* Maria

da Conceição Tavares de Castro. So there was no problem in issuing her with a passport. Her nineteen-year-old partner, Paul Miny, on the other hand, was from Luxembourg. To make their Portuguese passport more believable, Sousa Mendes had no compunction in committing a forgery: he registered Paul as Maria's brother.

On 7 June 1940, the Portuguese secret police informed the Foreign Ministry that three Polish nationals had been arrested in Vilar Formoso in possession of passports containing visas signed by Sousa Mendes on 29 May.

Aristides had seen Andrée again. She was expecting a baby by him – which was hardly surprising since, when she left her home in Ribérac more than a year earlier, she had announced: 'When I come back, I'll be pregnant!' She made a triumphant return one Sunday in the middle of the 11a.m. mass at Ribérac's church.

Pedro Nuno returned to Bordeaux to take his exams. José was also living at Quai Louis-XVIII. He had remained inconsolable ever since the death of his elder brother, Manuel. Meanwhile the German armies were advancing at top speed.

César was in Warsaw. During bombing raids, he organized prayers in the cellar of his block of flats. When everyone emerged afterwards, they found that the whole block had been destroyed except for their building. His neighbours pleaded with him to stay on.

From 20 May on, thousands of refugees began to pour

into Bordeaux. The city was about to become France's capital, or safe haven, for the third time in its history.

The first time was at the end of 1870, at the height of the Franco-Prussian War. A telegram from the Interior Ministry arrived at Bordeaux city hall: 'The special representative of the War Ministry and its administrative department are moving to your city, where they will arrive at about 6a.m. tomorrow. I would be obliged if you would make available to them the greatest possible number of rooms in the city hall, and in particular, if they are not being used at the moment, the apartments set aside for the reception of sovereigns.' The Second Empire had just collapsed.

'Paris was besieged on September 17, 1870,' writes Jean Chédaille,[3] 'and those leaders who were supposed to be last to leave the capital had temporarily set up their headquarters in Tours. But not for very long, since, according to a tradition that was fast establishing itself, hardly had you unpacked your bags when you packed them again, as soon as the Prussian troops got as far south as the highly symbolic site of the Château de Chambord.' On 8 December all politicians, civil servants and ministry staff were ordered to take the 10p.m. train from Tours to Bordeaux.

They arrived bleary-eyed in Bordeaux in the small hours of the morning. On 23 December, the government was received at the city hall by Bordeaux's municipal council. On the 28th, the Interior Minister, Léon Gambetta, who had left Paris in a balloon, also arrived at Bordeaux's Gare Saint-Jean. On 21 March, the Bordeaux assembly, which was made up of local worthies, ratified the armistice.

One month after the beginning of the 1914–18 war, Bordeaux once again became France's temporary capital. Forty-four years after Gambetta and Adolphe Thiers, President Raymond Poincaré moved into the prefecture building. At that time, 25,000–30,000 people from outside Bordeaux had taken refuge in the city. They left in January 1915, once the front had become stabilized.

'They' returned twenty-five years later, having been forced to take to the roads as the Nazi war machine swung into action. The refugees arrived in Bordeaux before the government ministers. They came in their tens of thousands from all over Europe. 'The hotels placarded "no vacancies",' writes Dominique Lormier, 'and some refugees slept in their vehicles.'[4]

'There were people sleeping everywhere,' notes Chédaille.[5] 'In cars, on benches, in the Gare Saint-Jean's subways, in public gardens.' A mass of women, children and old people found refuge in the station. Trains packed with refugees arrived all the time. Restaurants, bakeries and cafés were taken by storm. Place Pey-Berland became a car park for vehicles on their way to the south of France or Spain.

A permanent traffic jam of gigantic proportions blocked the Pont de Pierre. There was an indescribable crush of buses, carts, lorries and cars packed with passengers and weighed down with beds and chairs on their roofs. A Bordeaux painter, Charles Philippe, immortalized the scene in a celebrated etching. The city's port was also very busy, with no fewer than 400 boats putting in during the month of June alone.

During the night of 13–14 June, the date planned by Hitler, the Germans entered Paris. Adriano Moreira, a future minister under Salazar and then a student in Lisbon, remembers: 'When we heard that Paris had fallen, emotions ran deep. I was at the theatre that evening. A very popular actress came on stage carrying a French flag. When she sang *La Madelon*, many people started crying. It was a time when French was very much Portugal's second language, and everything that was good came from France.' Children who were curious about their origins would be told: 'You came from France in a wicker basket.'

On 14 June 1940, then, Bordeaux once again became the capital of France, a country that had just suffered the worst defeat in its history. A line of official cars crossed the Pont de Pierre during the evening. The Romanian ambassador had to spend two nights sleeping in his car before finding accommodation. Marshal Philippe Pétain and Pierre Laval moved into the city hall. General Maxime Weygand stayed in the Rue Vital-Carles, and General Charles de Gaulle at the Hôtel Majestic, a stone's throw from the Quai Louis-XVIII.

From his window, the man who two days later would leave for London could perhaps see the huge queue of

1. Aristides de Sousa Mendes

2. Passal, the Sousa Mendes home at Cabanas de Viriato

3. José de Sousa Mendes and his wife, Maria Angelina, with their sons, José Paulo (*front*), Aristides and César

4. Aristides and César de Sousa Mendes (circled) when law students at
Coimbra University in 1907

5. Aristides and César de Sousa
Mendes in 1907

6. The first official photograph of
Aristides de Sousa Mendes in
diplomatic dress in 1910

7. Aristides de Sousa Mendes and his wife,
Angelina, in 1911

8. César de Sousa Mendes and his wife, Maria Luísa, in Japan in 1915

9. Aristides de Sousa Mendes in Zanzibar in 1915. He is wearing a sultan's ceremonial dress

10. Aristides and Angelina de Sousa Mendes in Zanzibar in 1917 with their children: (*from left*) Aristides, José, Manuel, Isabel, Geraldo and Clotilde

11. César and Aristides de Sousa Mendes in the 1920s

12. The Sousa Mendes family in Berkeley, California, in 1923

13. Angelina de Sousa Mendes and her ten children on their way from California to Brazil in 1924

14. The 'Expresso dos Montes Hermínios' (a Ford vehicle customized to accommodate the whole family) after its crash in 1939

refugees who were waiting in front of the Portuguese consulate in the hope of getting the visa that might save their lives.
The Nazi armies were on their way, and anyone with a
Jewish name or a record of having fought totalitarianism had
at all costs to get out of France as quickly as possible.

César de Sousa Mendes, the son of Aristides's twin brother,
César, arrived in Bordeaux at that time. 'When I arrived in
the city and went to the Portuguese consulate,' he remembers, 'I immediately noticed a huge crowd of refugees head-
ing in the direction of the consulate. The closer I got to the
building, the denser the crowd became. [. . .] There were
lots of old and sick people [. . .], pregnant women who
were unwell, defenceless people who had seen their parents
machine-gunned on the roads by aircraft.'

What most struck César when he entered the building on
the Quai Louis-XVIII was the fact that there were also
refugees in the offices and part of Aristides de Sousa Mendes's
private apartment, sleeping on chairs, on the bare floor or
on blankets.

'Even the consulate offices were packed with refugees,'
he remembers. 'They were dead tired, because they had
spent days and nights in the street, on the stairs and finally in
the offices. They could no longer relieve themselves or eat
or drink, for fear of losing their place in the queue. That
sometimes happened and caused scuffles. The refugees
consequently looked haggard, and were no longer able to
wash, comb their hair, shave or change their clothes. In most

cases, anyway, the clothes they were wearing were the only ones they had.'

Again according to César, the incidents got so out of hand that the army had to be called in to keep order. Several soldiers under the orders of a sergeant bivouacked in the offices.

There were more surprises in store for César. When he entered the apartment, he found his two cousins, Pedro Nuno and José, and his aunt, Angelina. They were all extremely worried: Aristides had taken to his bed the previous day and not left it since, not even to eat. He alternated between a state of great agitation, as though he were suffering from a high temperature, and one of dazed prostration.

'What's going on here?' César asked.

4. 'From now on, there will be no more nationalities, races or religions'

As soon as they arrived in Bordeaux at the end of May 1940, many refugees headed straight for the Portuguese consulate, for they knew that a visa for Lisbon would provide them with an escape route. Others, who were less well informed and could think only of getting out of the city before the Nazis arrived, got swept along by the crowd that was beginning to flock to the consulate.

Some of them had heard that the Portuguese consul was particularly sympathetic to their plight. As we have seen, on several occasions since the beginning of May, Aristides de Sousa Mendes had already ignored Circular 14, which spelled out [the Portuguese government's] new regulations governing the issuing of visas. News of his attitude had filtered out to the refugees. More and more of them naturally started applying for visas. Had he decided to respect Circular 14 to the letter, Sousa Mendes would have had to ask the Portuguese Foreign Ministry in writing for permission to issue virtually every visa. That requirement, which was difficult enough to satisfy at the best of times, had become quite impossible given the situation in Bordeaux in the early summer of 1940.

Sousa Mendes had notified the Portuguese authorities of that situation on several occasions. On 21 May, he sent a telegram to Salazar requesting instructions on how to deal with the flood of refugees. The answer was curt: enforce Circular 14. On 13 June, the government refused to issue the visas which Sousa Mendes had requested for some thirty people.

One of them was Rabbi Chaim Kruger. Sousa Mendes had met him in front of a synagogue which was to become the scene of a bloody crackdown by Nazi troops two years later. The two men, who had been brought together by a quirk of history, immediately became the firmest of friends.

The only thing the Catholic and monarchist Portuguese aristocrat and the rabbi from Antwerp had in common was that they were both good men in evil times. There is a striking photograph that shows them both in Lisbon a few months later: the rabbi, who has a long beard and is wearing a black hat and a buttoned-up overcoat, is as gaunt as Sousa Mendes is corpulent. With his unruly grey hair, protruding belly, loosely knotted bow-tie and round spectacles, Sousa Mendes had changed a lot since the moment when he first entered the Foreign Ministry in ceremonial dress. He may have become a little stouter, but there is a much more powerful aura of humanity about him.

'One day in mid-May, our father said to us: "We've got

to get out of Antwerp!"' says Ann Ehrenfeld, Rabbi Kruger's daughter. 'It was a Monday. We went to the railway station and managed to board a train full of refugees that had come from the German border.'

Rabbi Kruger's son, Jacob, picks up the story: 'When Aristides de Sousa Mendes met my father, he immediately offered us hospitality. Just imagine: at the height of the war, he invited a man he had never met before into his home – on top of which we were Jews!'

The Krugers moved into Sousa Mendes's apartment on Quai Louis-XVIII. There was plenty of room, as only two of his children, Pedro Nuno and José, were there at the time. Sousa Mendes applied for visas for the rabbi and his family. As we have seen, a negative response came on 13 June. Sousa Mendes promised his friend he would do everything in his power to get him the precious visas that would allow him to leave France with his family. The rabbi then said something that had a radical effect on Sousa Mendes: 'It's not just me that needs help, but all my fellow Jews who are in danger of their lives.'

The Jews were indeed in danger. Most of those who failed to escape would end up in concentration camps, after suffering the humiliation of the first anti-Jewish measures introduced by the Vichy regime. The yellow star that they had sewn on to the whole family's clothing one evening would turn them into different human beings next day when they opened the shop or went to school, the factory or the office. And then there was the ban on frequenting public places: a large Bordeaux café put up a notice which read 'No Jews or dogs.'

They would scurry along the street with their eyes on the ground, feeling a knot in their stomach every time they passed German soldiers. Then one day they were rounded up at dawn by French policemen and taken in cattle trucks to the Drancy transit camp in the suburbs of Paris. Their final destination – the camps – left them no chance.

Eighty-five-year-old Rabbi Marcel Stourdze appeared as a witness at the trial of Maurice Papon in 1998. Papon, a former prefect of the Paris police and former budget minister, was found guilty of complicity with crimes against humanity: as a senior official at the Bordeaux prefecture in 1943, he had approved the deportation of Jews to Germany.

'Just try to imagine what deportation was like,' Stourdze told the jury. 'We arrived at the Auschwitz camp. We were told to take off all our clothes. A deportee came to shave us – the armpits, chest hair, pubic hair. Another deportee brought a bucket with a mixture of water and paraffin in it to get rid of any lice we might have. Imagine, ladies, being sponged all over your body, on your breasts, between your legs! We were each given a number, which a deportee then tattooed on us. He had a penholder with a pin in it. He tapped the skin not with the pointed end but with the pinhead. He made holes for the figures. Ten holes were needed to form one figure. We had become nothing but a number.'

The men and women waiting outside the Portuguese consulate were potential numbers. They were not refugees, but people under sentence of death. Naturally neither Sousa Mendes nor Rabbi Kruger could imagine the unimaginable, the total horror of the Holocaust. Yet Kruger had told his friend: 'My fellow Jews are in danger of their lives.'

Pedro Nuno, who was present during the conversation, remembers: 'All of a sudden my father seemed terribly weary, as though he had been struck down by a violent disease. He just looked at us and went to bed.'

Sebastião Mendes, the son known as 'the American' by his brothers and sisters, was not in Bordeaux at the time. But in *A Flight through Hell*, a short story based on accounts by various people which he published in 1951 under the pseudonym 'Michael d'Avranches',[1] he painted a striking portrait of his father at this crucial point in his life. 'He looked grave, his eyes had blue circles around them. His hair had turned completely grey, as white as snow almost.'

That was the atmosphere that César de Sousa Mendes, Aristides's nephew, discovered on his arrival at the apartment on Quai Louis-XVIII. Thousands of refugees were waiting outside, guarded by uniformed soldiers. In his bedroom Sousa Mendes tossed and turned on his bed, sweating profusely and occasionally groaning. Despite the agony he was going through, he refused any help from his family. He remained in that state for three days and nights. During that period Sousa Mendes had no contact with the outside world.

On the morning of the fourth day (16 June), everything suddenly changed.

'My father got up, having apparently recovered his serenity,' Pedro Nuno remembers. 'He was full of punch. He washed, shaved and got dressed. Then he strode out of his bedroom, flung open the door to the chancellery, and announced in a loud voice: "From now on I'm giving everyone visas. There will be no more nationalities, races or religions." Then our father told us that he had heard a voice, that of his conscience or of God, which dictated to him what course of action he should take, and that everything was perfectly clear in his mind.'

César remembers other things his uncle said: 'I cannot allow all you people to die. Many of you are Jews, and our constitution clearly states that neither the religion nor the political beliefs of foreigners can be used as a pretext for refusing to allow them to stay in Portugal. I've decided to be faithful to that principle, but I shan't resign for all that. The only way I can respect my faith as a Christian is to act in accordance with the dictates of my conscience.'

On 16 June 1940, at Quai Louis-XVIII in Bordeaux, there began what Yehuda Bauer, one of the most eminent historians of that period, has described as 'the greatest rescue operation carried out by a single person during the Holocaust'.

As Sousa Mendes, mainly with the help of Rabbi Kruger, got down to the task of signing visa after visa, events were gathering pace elsewhere. At 4p.m. Charles de Gaulle, who had gone on a lightning visit to London, reported to the French council of ministers on a British offer to form a joint government with France.

The meeting was stormy. Crowds in the street gave vent to their anti-parliamentary feelings. Paul Reynaud stepped down as prime minister and, at 10p.m., President Albert Lebrun asked Marshal Philippe Pétain to form a new government. It was to be the last cabinet meeting of the Third Republic.

Sousa Mendes spent the whole day signing visas. He applied the principle of 'no questions asked'. He cared not a bit about the applicants' religion, nationality or ethnic origin. He just kept on signing.

That day, while an industrial and scientific machine designed to annihilate a whole people was being methodically set up in France and other countries, the Portuguese consul in Bordeaux was putting into practice Terence's maxim: I am a man, and nothing pertaining to man is alien to me.

To speed things up, Sousa Mendes set up a veritable assembly line. Often it would be Rabbi Kruger who went to fetch the passports. He asked his fellow Jews who were on the stairs or in the street to hand over their identity papers.

The rabbi's son, who was present at the time, remembers: 'He was carrying fistfuls of passports. But the most extraordinary thing was that he was so engrossed in his task, so keen to act fast and save as many people as he could, that he went out into the street without his black jacket, without his hat and even without his skullcap – something I'd never seen him do before.' Once the passports were on the table, Aristides signed them and José Seabra, the consular secretary, rubber-stamped them.

Seabra was not exactly overjoyed to be taking part in such a blatant, brazen and repeated violation of the regulations. He was torn between his awestruck respect for the rules and regulations and a genuine affection for the consul and approval of the actions they were taking, which he knew were generous-hearted. He tried to dissuade Sousa Mendes: 'For the sake of your wife and children, please stop! You're ruining your life and that of your family.'

Seabra's efforts were in vain. Yet he tried to maintain a semblance of legality in what he probably regarded as a madhouse. From the start, he painstakingly wrote, in a neat, flowing hand, the names of all visa recipients in a large ledger. He also tried to get people to keep to certain hours. He would get gently rapped over the knuckles for this by Sousa Mendes, who jokingly called out to visa applicants whom Seabra refused to let in: 'Come back when the dictator is not here!'

While Pedro Nuno, true to his Christian faith, totally approved of his father's actions and helped him as best he could – when he was not preparing for his exams – the other Sousa Mendes children were much less enthusiastic. José, still overcome with grief and bitterness [at the death of his elder brother, Manuel], tried to escape reality by playing the piano.

His elder sister, Isabel, arrived in Bordeaux with her husband, Jules d'Aout. Although they wanted to flee from the Germans and reach the safety of Portugal, the couple could not understand Aristides's reasons either. They thought he was taking unnecessary risks. Isabel pressed her point: 'You must stop, Father! Stop taking so many risks! You ought to think of your future and ours.' They turned out to be no more persuasive than Seabra – and were roped in by Aristides to help in the signing of visas. César also lent a hand.

Angelina, as discreet and as admirably selfless as ever, tried to keep the household working normally. As she was without servants, she herself had to tend to all the people who flocked to the consulate, helping a child, comforting a mother, or giving an old man a glass of water.

The drawing-room and dining-room had been invaded by refugees, so it was in the kitchen that members of the family snatched a bite to eat whenever they could. The consulate's doors were no longer locked. 'One night, a little girl of eight who had come on her own asked us what she should do in order to escape,' Pedro Nuno recalls. 'She said her parents had been machine-gunned. She had supper with us in the kitchen. She showed us an envelope with a diamond in it and wanted to give it to us. My father said to her: "Quick, hide that in your pocket!" Next day she was taken care of by other refugees and we never saw her again.'

On 17 June, the news that the Portuguese consul was issuing everyone with visas spread like wildfire among the crowds of refugees in Bordeaux. The apartment was taken by storm.

During the night, the Spanish ambassador had passed on France's request for an armistice to the Germans. At midday, Pétain spoke on French radio: 'I make to France the gift of my person, to attenuate her suffering. [. . .] It is with a heavy heart that I say to you today that the combat must cease.' Next day, a journalist on the Bordeaux newspaper, *La Petite Gironde*, wrote: 'He finished his announcement. Strains of *La Marseillaise* filled the room. The diners rose to their feet. Then there was a long silence. Some women wept. The men gritted their teeth.'

That same day, Georges Mandel, a minister in the outgoing government, who was regarded as Clemenceau's spiritual heir, was arrested on the grounds that he had taken part in an alleged plot. Once freed, he was taken to see Pétain, and instead of thanking him he said: 'I pity you, I pity you. I mean I commiserate with you, and I pity my country, which has taken you as its leader!' Pétain wrote him a letter of apology, which was found in Mandel's pocket when he was murdered by the collaborationist Vichy Milices on 7 July 1944.

Another event on that same day went unnoticed: de Gaulle took off from Mérignac airfield, on the outskirts of Bordeaux, bound for London. As Winston Churchill was to write, de Gaulle alone 'carried with him, in this small aeroplane, the honour of France'.

The German troops had reached Dijon. While Sousa Mendes continued signing visas in the sweltering summer heat, the staff of other embassies were 'living it up', as Jean Chédaille remarks ironically.[2] They homed in on the top wine-producing châteaux: Soviet diplomats stayed at Château Ducru-Beaucaillou, for example, and the Monegasques at Château La Gaffelière. The Swiss preferred Château Guiraud, in the Sauternes region.

'Bordeaux could be described as drunk and disorderly,' Chédaille goes on. 'Allées de Tourny, Place de la Comédie, Cours du Chapeau-Rouge and Rue Esprit-des-Lois were a solid mass of traffic. There were people driving in every direction. Traffic jams formed, then melted away. More cars arrived all the time and got sucked into the extraordinary maelstrom. [. . .] It took more than an hour to get from the Côte des Pavillons to the Pont de Pierre. The railway station was just as congested. There were trains full of refugees at every platform. The railway staff worked wonders. The thirty security police on duty at Saint-Jean were at their wit's end. Bordeaux had become the capital of chaos.'

When Pedro Nuno came back from the university in mid-afternoon, there were such huge and dense crowds in front of No. 14 Quai Louis-XVIII that he had difficulty in getting into his own home. As he elbowed his way through the crowd, he did his best to explain: 'Let me through, please,

I live here, I'm the consul's son.' When he at last managed to reach the first floor of the consulate, he found his father signing visa after visa with the help of Seabra, Kruger, Isabel and Jules. He too knuckled down to the task.

Aristides was exhausted. His weariness, combined with his determination to act more and more swiftly so as to save as many people as possible, forced him to abbreviate his signature. He no longer had time to write 'Aristides de Sousa Mendes' with a fine flourish of the pen. He now simply signed 'Mendes' and said, 'Next person please.'

The next person might be a Jew from Lille, a stateless person from Riga, a diamond merchant from Antwerp, a retired person from Juvisy or a bourgeois from Prague. But wherever they had come from, they were all united by the same determination, the same aim and the same fear. They could think of nothing but putting as much distance as possible between them and the barbarous armies whose dark shadow was spreading across Europe.

Later, Sousa Mendes explained why he had acted as he had. In a letter to his government, he wrote that his aim was indeed to save all the refugees: 'Their suffering cannot be expressed in words: some had lost their wives, others had no news of their children, and others again had seen their loved ones die during German bombing raids.'

He went on: 'There was something else that could not be ignored: the fate that awaited all those people should they fall into the hands of the enemy.' Here was Sousa Mendes using the word 'enemy'. Whereas the government in Lisbon – his government – talked in terms of neutrality, Sousa Mendes showed he had decided which side he was on. He explained that among the refugees there were officers from occupied countries like Austria, Czechoslovakia and Poland, who would have been shot as rebels had they fallen into German hands.

Sousa Mendes then admitted that, as the father of many children himself, he had been 'terribly upset' by the splitting up of families. 'My attitude,' he concluded, 'was motivated solely by feelings of altruism and generosity, of which the Portuguese, during the eight centuries of their history, have so often given eloquent proof.'

He knew he was disobeying. His action brings to mind the attitude of St-Heran, one of the provincial commanders who was ordered by Charles IX to kill all Protestants in 1572, and who replied: 'Sir, I have received an order under your majesty's seal to put to death all the Protestants in my province. I have too much respect for your majesty not to believe that the letter is a forgery; and if, God forbid, the order has indeed come from your majesty, I still have too much respect for you to obey you.'

That admirable reply, which was quoted by the barrister Arno Klarsfeld during the trial of Maurice Papon in 1998, is the kind of answer that Sousa Mendes might have given Salazar: I respect your excellency too much to apply Circular 14.

Many important figures were able to obtain visas thanks to Sousa Mendes. César describes how a French ambassador 'threw himself on his knees and begged' his uncle to grant him and his family visas, pointing out that he had daughters he wanted to save. 'It was midday,' César recalls, 'and my uncle, my aunt and myself were having lunch in the kitchen when the ambassador turned up. [. . .] My uncle, as considerate as ever, broke off his meal, even though it was the only time of day when he could hope to be alone with his family.'

Another family was given special help by Sousa Mendes, that of the Flemish politician, Albert de Vleeschauwer. The two men took to each other immediately. De Vleeschauwer had taught, and Sousa Mendes lived, in Louvain for some years, but they had apparently not made each other's acquaintance there. They were both devout Catholics and convinced royalists.

It was Jules d'Aout, Aristides's son-in-law, who brought the two men together. Jules, his wife Isabel and their two-year-old son, Manuel, had arrived in Bordeaux with two friends of theirs. The three men had just graduated from the School of Colonial Administration and wanted to become administrators in the Belgian Congo or in Rwanda-Burundi. From the very beginning of the war they had hoped to set off for the colonies. De Vleeschauwer, who was then Minister of Colonies, advised them to travel to Lisbon, and then take a boat from there to the Congo.

When de Vleeschauwer arrived in Bordeaux, he was appointed by the Belgian government, then on its last legs (or rather appointed himself), 'general administrator of the Congo' with full powers. Never before in Belgium's constitutional history had an ordinary minister been invested with such responsibilities.

Sousa Mendes realized the political significance of his new friend's appointment, which could prevent the Belgian colonies from falling into the hands of the Germans. Out of friendship and generosity, as well as political intuition, he offered to put up the whole de Vleeschauwer family at Cabanas de Viriato [his home village in Portugal], thus allowing the new administrator of the Congo to prepare himself for his task in a more serene frame of mind.

On 17 June, it was past 10p.m. when the exhausted Sousa Mendes finally got to bed.

The next day, as the sun rose over the Quai Louis-XVIII, Aristides and his team, who had by then got into their stride, went back to work. Seabra, even though he was keen to continue giving the operation a semblance of legality, had given up writing the names of all the visa recipients in the consulate's ledger. As though to justify himself, he wrote in it: 'Visas have been issued outside opening hours.' The previous day, he had already decided to stop asking refugees to pay the visa registration fees.

The crowds were just as large and motley as on the previous two days, except that they had perhaps become a little more edgy as the Germans moved closer and the French authorities prepared to opt for collaboration. There was less and less time to be lost.

It is edifying to look at the register today and note the names of those who were granted visas. The entry for 18 June alone, for example, shows such names as Langevin, Weinberg, Vermeesch, Bloch, Kauffmann, Frisch, Levy, García, Smith and Pearce. Number 1436 was Robert Montgomery: the celebrated Hollywood actor also owed a great debt of gratitude to Sousa Mendes. As did Edouard, Henri and Robert de Rothschild, all of whom obtained visas from the consulate on Quai Louis-XVIII.

Archduke Otto of Habsburg, a descendant of one of Europe's most illustrious families, sent his private secretary, Henry Count Degenfeld, to the consulate to pick up visas.

Habsburg, a man of great wit who, when told once by an aide about a forthcoming Austria–Hungary football match, replied: 'And who are we playing against?' remains sprightly today despite his eighty-six years. Comfortably ensconced in his European Parliament office in Strasbourg, he remembers those tragic days in 1940.

It should be remembered that Hitler, an Austrian, hated the Habsburg family. He lambasted them in *Mein Kampf*: their mere existence was an obstacle in the way of his great dream – which he unfortunately realized – of annexing Austria (Anschluss). Nor had Hitler ever forgiven the young

Otto of Habsburg – who, incidentally, studied at Louvain University for a time – for having refused more than once to meet him.

After fleeing to Paris, Habsburg not only campaigned against the Nazis but used his savoir-faire to assist compatriots of his who had become refugees. 'Several thousand Austrians, including many Jews (100,000 Jews fled from Austria between March 1938 and May 1939), settled in France,' writes Jean Sévilla in his biography of Otto of Habsburg's mother, Empress Zita of Austria.[3]

'I had done a lot of negotiating with Daladier [when he was prime minister],' Habsburg remembers. 'I wanted fall-back zones to be created for refugees if war broke out. But it was above all Georges Mandel [Minister of the Interior], a real gentleman, who helped me. When the front line caved in, we were all amazed. We could never have imagined that France would collapse like that. A few days before the Germans entered Paris, I dined at the Ritz with an American diplomat. We were alone in the patio, and we could see the sky being lit up by the fighting that was going on around the capital.' Sévilla notes that the signature that comes immediately after Habsburg's in the Ritz's visitors' book is that of Marshal Erwin Rommel.

Otto of Habsburg, his mother, Empress Zita, and his grandmother, the Duchess of Parma, first took refuge at a château belonging to their cousin, Xavier de Bourbon, near Moulins in central France. It was there that Otto received a telephone call from Mandel, who told him that he and several other members of parliament were going to leave for Morocco and start a resistance movement there. Then, at the Château de Lamonzie-Montastruc, they joined the family of the Grand Duchess of Luxembourg, who had refused to collaborate with the Germans and also obtained visas from Quai Louis-XVIII.

Otto of Habsburg, his brother Charles and Count Degenfeld immediately travelled to Bordeaux to meet a number of highly placed people. In a letter of 18 May 1968 to Aristides de Sousa Mendes's daughter Joana, Count Degenfeld gave a detailed account of those days in Bordeaux, after paying a particularly warm tribute to Sousa Mendes.

'It became immediately clear,' he wrote, 'that the government would ask for an armistice, and that in that case the imperial family would be in danger to be [sic] handed over to the Germans, if no escape was made before.'

On 17 June, Degenfeld went to the Portuguese consulate, where 'an immense number of people' were pushing to get in. He was taken in to see Sousa Mendes, who asked him to come back as soon as possible with all the imperial family's passports. 'I therefore went at ten o'clock in the evening again to the consulate,' Degenfeld went on in his letter to Joana, 'and your father, although evidently very tired from the immense work he had done all during this day and the previous ones, put personally all the visas on the nineteen passports I presented him and signed them. I could in these short minutes highly appreciate the noble feelings of your father who had decided to help as many of the refugees as possible to escape the German danger.'

Degenfeld, who said that the refugees included many Austrians, both Jewish and non-Jewish, that had fled Nazism, then asked Sousa Mendes if he could also issue visas to a number of Austrian nationals who had been working for Austria in France for two years. Sousa Mendes agreed, and the Quai Louis-XVIII team received several hundred extra passports to sign.

Otto of Habsburg and his family left for Portugal. The Germans asked Salazar to extradite them. Salazar made it clear to Otto that he would not agree to that request, but asked him to leave Lisbon as quickly as possible. The imperial family then flew to the United States. There, Otto again tried to get visas granted to his compatriots. He was bitterly disappointed at the response he got from a very senior Washington diplomat: 'There are enough Jews here already. Let Hitler keep the rest!'

He was pleasantly surprised, on the other hand, by the response he received from some Central American dictators, such as General Rafael Trujillo Molina of the Dominican Republic, who granted 3,000 visas.

Although Otto of Habsburg never met Aristides de Sousa Mendes, he has fond memories of his action. And when I pointed out to him that he too had saved the lives of several thousand people, he gave a truly regal answer: 'I was only doing my duty, whereas what Sousa Mendes accomplished was an admirable action.'

On the evening of 18 June, only a few people in Bordeaux were able to pick up the BBC in London when it broadcast a message from an unknown general called Charles de Gaulle, who became France's first resistant. He told them that their country had lost a battle but not the war, and called upon them not to give in: 'France is not alone! Whatever happens, the flame of the French Resistance must not and will not be put out.' The government's reaction came swiftly. General Louis Colson, the War Minister, 'recalled' de Gaulle, as though he had gone AWOL.

On 19 June, the flow of refugees seemed to ease off slightly. But Sousa Mendes went on signing visas. Then he took a short break to meet the American writer Eugene Bagger at the Café Splendid. That evening, de Gaulle made a second broadcast that was much harder-hitting than that of the previous day, particularly as regards the French government. His call for people to resist was also much more clear-cut. British diplomats were still in Bordeaux trying to extract a promise from the government that it would not allow the French fleet to fall into German hands.

'The weather continued to be set fair, but the situation was less so,' Chédaille writes. 'Journalists noted that, from the morning of June 19 on, the people of Bordeaux started queuing in Place Pierre-Lafitte (which after the war was renamed Place Jean-Moulin, after the Resistance hero) in front of the offices of the Caisse d'Epargne savings bank (now the Musée Jean-Moulin). As investments were at risk, people were withdrawing their money, and commenting on recent events as they did so. [. . .] There were still as many people as before, [. . .] still as many cars from else-where, parked all over the place, sometimes apparently aban-doned. [. . .] The machinery of administrative and civilian life continued to function normally. Verdicts were handed down in the law courts; exams were being held at the university; and *Snow White and the Seven Dwarfs* was showing at the cinema.'[4]

That same day, further to the south, a strange convoy of vehicles crossed the bridge between Hendaye and Irún that marks the border between France and Spain. Their passen-gers included Empress Zita of Austria, Otto of Habsburg and their retinue, and the de Vleeschauwers.

Elsa Van Overstraeten, Albert de Vleeschauwer's daugh-ter, remembers: 'I was twelve. It was the unhappiest day of my life. My father, who in the meantime had gone to London, had bidden us farewell, saying: "The war will last a long time, but we'll win it!" I had no idea when I would see him again, so you can imagine my despair.'

Three families, including a total of twenty-two children, travelled all the way to Lisbon in two lorries and three cars. The ex-minister and new general administrator of the Congo wanted to help the family of de Schrijver, who had founded the Flemish Social Christian Party, as well as reserve captain Alfred Raport, or 'Uncle Alfred', who was an old friend of his.

The convoy also included Isabel and Jules d'Aout and their first child, Manuel. 'We had also taken along with us,' says Ludovic de Vleeschauwer, one of Albert's sons, 'a friend of the family, Miss Rosa Delerue, who was the first Flemish woman student at Louvain University, and one of her friends, a Dominican friar, Edouard Van Rooy, who taught theology in Rome and had taken a radical stance against racism – and who had no idea where to go.' The journey took several days.

Aristides had remained in Bordeaux with Angelina, his two sons, Pedro Nuno and José, and his nephew, César. That night the Luftwaffe bombed Bordeaux. The raid took a heavy toll: more than eighty people were killed, 100 or so were wounded and there was considerable material damage.

At the height of the bombing a curious figure turned up at Sousa Mendes's apartment: Charles Oulmont, a writer and professor at the Sorbonne. 'He moved into my uncle's home,' César remembers. 'He ate with us in the kitchen and slept in one of the bedrooms. From the moment he entered the house, he never wore anything but pyjamas. He lived in mortal fear of being caught by the Nazis – but his fear was justified, since he had criticized the Hitler regime in print.

He was immensely wealthy: he had four potato sacks full of solid gold. In the hope of persuading my uncle to grant him a visa, he promised him half his fortune. My uncle turned the offer down, but gave him his visa.'

That made one more visa. But it was by no means to be the last.

5. 'I'll save you all!'

Aristides de Sousa Mendes did not stop at that. During World War II most diplomats, whether Portuguese or not, obeyed their government's orders from the start and therefore granted visas only sparingly, preferring to wait quietly for the war to end.

A minority among them, for humanitarian or political reasons, showed a little more generosity and allowed certain stateless persons to leave France. A few dozen diplomats heeded their conscience more than their career plan and helped those who could be helped. And a small handful of hotheads went even further and deliberately disobeyed so as to prevent thousands of people from being massacred.

The best-known of these was the Swede Raoul Wallenberg, who issued diplomatic papers to more than 30,000 Hungarian Jews, thus preventing them from being deported to Auschwitz. Varian Fry, an American diplomat posted in Marseille, granted visas to more than 2,500 Jews in 1940 against the advice of his government. Those he saved included many intellectuals, artists, writers and scientists, such as Marc Chagall, Max Ernst, André Breton and Thomas Mann's brother, Heinrich Mann.

There was George Duckwitz, too, a trade attaché at the German embassy in Copenhagen and member of the Nazi Party, who risked his life by warning the Danes that Hitler intended to deport Danish Jews and thus enabled almost all of them to be evacuated to Sweden. Feng Shan Ho, China's consul general in Vienna, issued thousands of visas to Austrian Jews without any authorization, thus allowing them to flee to Shanghai.

Carl Lutz, the Swiss consul in Budapest, permitted almost 10,000 Jewish children to depart for Palestine, and then, in liaison with Wallenberg, saved tens of thousands of other people as well. Chiune Sugihara, the Japanese consul in Lithuania, saved more than 10,000 Polish Jews. And Jan Zwartendijk, the Dutch consul in Lithuania, granted almost 2,000 people visas to go to the Dutch colony of Surinam.

Aristides de Sousa Mendes undoubtedly belongs to this confraternity of heroic diplomats, who alone saved the lives of more than 200,000 people.

By the morning of 20 June, the atmosphere at Quai Louis-XVIII had become less chaotic than it had been over the previous three days: armed with their visas, thousands of refugees had been able to leave Bordeaux. It was also less anxious: Isabel and Jules d'Aout had left with their son,

Manuel; and Pedro Nuno and José had also returned to Portugal. But Professor Oulmont was still there, and still in the same state of terror.

Satisfied that he had done his duty and obeyed his conscience, Sousa Mendes might legitimately have been expected to rest at last from his labours. But when he had said 'I will save you all!' he meant it. There still remained an enormous amount to be done.

Although the main task in Bordeaux had been accomplished, he was needed farther south. In Toulouse, Bayonne and Hendaye, thousands more refugees were waiting to find a way of getting out of France. They were increasingly anxious and afraid. The Nazi flag had cast its evil shadow over virtually the whole of France.

Sousa Mendes had already authorized Portugal's honorary vice-consul in Toulouse, Emile Gissot, who was French, to issue visas himself, although he was not strictly empowered to do so. He did so because thousands of refugees in that city were waiting to leave France.

Pressure was mounting all the time. Then came the news, also on 20 June, that the *Massilia* had sailed from Bordeaux with twenty-seven members of parliament on board, who had decided to leave France and take refuge in Morocco. They included Mandel, Daladier, André Le Troquer and the young Pierre Mendès France, a future prime minister.

That same day, the British embassy in Lisbon wrote a

curious letter to the Portuguese Foreign Ministry in which it denounced the activity of Sousa Mendes, accusing him of working outside normal hours and of requesting extra fees for the issue of visas. Although apparently insignificant, the letter was to have unwelcome consequences.

Meanwhile Sousa Mendes was *en route* for Bayonne, accompanied by Professor Oulmont. He had to act swiftly, first because the Germans were getting closer and thousands of waiting refugees had to be saved, and secondly because he knew the Portuguese government was not going to allow him to 'disobey' for much longer.

Also on 20 June, on the basis of the British embassy's complaint, Salazar asked for steps to be taken to counter Sousa Mendes's action. 'Irregularities' committed by the consul in Bordeaux before war had even been declared were beginning to be reported. An emissary from the Portuguese embassy in Paris, which had also been transferred to a Bordeaux château, Château Lamarselle in St-Emilion, was asked to investigate what was going on at Quai Louis-XVIII.

This marked the beginning of a horrendous and tragic race against time between Sousa Mendes, the Portuguese authorities and the German armies. Now that the Spanish authorities had sealed off their borders and stopped issuing visas, now that the French population was on the point of accepting a collaborationist regime, now that the French police were about to join in the great hunt, the only hope for legions of refugees was to obtain a visa that would enable them to reach Lisbon via Spain.

That is why they set up camp in their thousands in front of the Portuguese consulates in Toulouse, Hendaye and Bayonne. What they did not realize was that because of Circular 14 the vast majority of them had no chance of obtaining a visa. The trap had closed behind them.

Some of the thousands of people who were issued visas by Aristides de Sousa Mendes were determined, fifty years later, to identify themselves so as to pay tribute to his memory. Alix Deguise was fifteen in June 1940. Her mother, Helena Hamburger, who was of Dutch origin, lived in Monaco. When Italy entered the war, she decided to go to the United States with her parents and her two children, Alix and her brother. When they arrived in Biarritz, they met a group of people, many of them Dutch, who were also trying to leave. Even today, Alix remembers that the group included a Cuban driven to desperation because he could no longer find any cigars. They had managed to lay their hands on an ordinary sardine boat, which had a motor as well as sails and could therefore take them to Spain. But the Spanish consulate refused to grant them visas. There were more than forty people in the group.

A man who had taken it upon himself to act as their leader had heard about Sousa Mendes and set off for Bayonne with all their passports. When he returned, he announced triumphantly: 'I've got all the visas!' The group set off on a voyage that lasted a week, and managed to reach Oporto, after putting in at Santander, where the Dutch consul threatened to have them arrested if they set foot on dry land. In Oporto, they boarded a Greek boat that took them across the Atlantic. Those on board included the Austrian writer Franz Werfel, his wife Alma (Gustav Mahler's widow), and Thomas Mann's brother, Heinrich.

'How I would have loved to have met Aristides de Sousa Mendes,' Deguise says today. She realizes she probably owes her life to him. The members of her family who stayed behind, such as her grandmother, uncle and great-uncle, were deported. Her grandmother died in a concentration camp.

In 1990, Manuel Dias, a Portuguese living in Bordeaux who took a close interest in the story of Sousa Mendes, arranged a rendezvous in Bayonne with Manoel Vieira Braga, who was the honorary Portuguese vice-consul in that town in 1940. They talked for a long time. Vieira Braga's account is fascinating.

'By the time Aristides de Sousa Mendes arrived in Bayonne, Salazar had asked for him to be arrested. I knew that,' Vieira Braga said. 'He too seemed to know that something was up. If he didn't actually know it was planned to arrest him, he realized that Lisbon was putting pressure on him. He struck me as both elated and aware of the situation. Like de Gaulle, he thought Germany would eventually lose the war. He also under-estimated the firmness of Salazar's grip on power and the Portuguese people's allegiance to him. But in any case he gave the impression of someone who was acting in a lucid and determined way.'

'Lucid' and 'determined' were very different epithets from those later used by other 'witnesses', such as Salazar's emissaries, who described Sousa Mendes as 'a crank and near madman'.

The situation Sousa Mendes found on his arrival in Bayonne was disastrous. The consulate was located on the third floor of a small, narrow building, at 8 Rue du Pilori. It could be reached only by a wooden staircase that was difficult to climb at the best of times.

A neighbour, Madame Chatillon Diharce, when interviewed by Diana Andringa's Portuguese television crew for her reportage, *O Cônsul Injustiçado* (*The Proscribed Consul*), said: 'There were so many people waiting both inside and outside the building that we were afraid the staircase would give way. The police tried to keep things under control. One day there were so many people crammed on the staircase that the vice-consul couldn't get past, so he was forced to come through our flat.'

In the same programme, Henri Zvi Deutsch, who was a child at the time, described how moved he was when he returned to Rue du Pilori: 'Coming down those stairs as my father and all the other refugees did, thinking of the mass of people who were there at the time, and realizing today that the staircase is only just wide enough for two people to stand on it side by side, I've now got a better idea of the time they must have spent there. I can just picture the expectations of those going up the stairs, and the joy of those coming down.'

Thérèse Torres-Levin, who was then eighteen and called Tereska Fzwarc, remembers: 'My uncle, who had gone to get visas for the whole family, was so jostled by the crowd that he tore his trousers.' She too realizes that she probably owes her life to Aristides de Sousa Mendes. 'I was living in Paris with my mother and grandparents. My father, who was Polish, had gone to London. One of my Polish cousins had arrived in Paris and told us what was going on in the Nazi-occupied countries, particularly as regards the Jews. He urged us to get out quickly.

'We then left for St-Jean-de-Luz. I even managed to take my *baccalauréat* exam in Bayonne. The Germans were on their way, and it wasn't easy to find a way of getting out of France. Luckily one of my uncles went to Bayonne and came back with the long-awaited visas – and his trousers torn. As we crossed the border with Spain at Irún, the Germans were just beginning to arrive. The French customs officer said to us with a growl: "They won't be staying long, the bastards!"'

The Germans eventually remained for four long years in France. After a short stay in Lisbon, Torres-Levin left to join the Free French Forces in London in October 1940.

The Portuguese consul in Bayonne, Faria Machado, was no professional diplomat. Since the exodus had started, he had been snowed under with visa applications. Since he wanted to stick scrupulously to the rules laid down by Lisbon, he was totally paralysed and kept on sending telegrams to his ministry requesting instructions.

His vice consul, Vieira Braga, was a small, well-dressed and extremely conservative man who apparently had more personality than his superior. Sousa Mendes was surprised to find the elderly and highly respected Portuguese ambassador in Brussels, Francisco de Calheiros e Meneses, at the consulate. He had come from Bordeaux, where he had taken refuge.

When he arrived at Rue du Pilori, Sousa Mendes had to force his way through the crowds of refugees. He climbed the wooden staircase. According to Sebastião, in *Flight through Hell*[1] (a version later confirmed by Vieira Braga), the following scene took place:

> The vice-consul came to inquire who we were and Dr Mendes, as he sat at one of the desks, inquired: 'Why do you not help those poor refugees?'
>
> 'Why, you know as well as I that our government has categorically refused to grant any visas to anybody. I am here to carry out the instructions I receive from my superiors.'
>
> 'How would you like to find yourself, your wife and children in the same circumstances as the refugees? You say you are here to carry out the instructions you receive from your superiors. Very well, I am still the consul at

Bordeaux and, consequently, your superior. I, therefore, order you to pass out as many visas as may be
needed.'

Vieira Braga, who feared, as he admitted later, that 'this
madness' would result in his being arrested by the French –
or German – authorities, and who was also afraid of having
to account for his acts to the government in Lisbon, tried, as
Seabra had done in Bordeaux, to convince Sousa Mendes
that he was taking a terrible risk. All to no avail. In Bordeaux,
Seabra had eventually agreed, out of admiration and affection
for 'his' consul, to help issue visas.

Things would seem to have turned out differently in
Bayonne, though the exact truth is difficult to establish even
today. Sousa Mendes later claimed that Faria Machado, Vieira
Braga and Calheiros e Meneses also signed visas. The three
men denied having done so, but there are some disturbing
contradictions in their testimony.

Once again Sousa Mendes set up a 'commando signing
operation' that lasted for three days and part of two nights. As
the armistice between France and Germany was about to be
concluded (it was signed on 22 June), there was no time to be
lost. Several thousand refugees were waiting in front of the
consulate, and the same number again, if not more, in the
centre of town. Every minute counted. As he had done during
his final days in Bordeaux, Sousa Mendes decided to stop asking for the fee normally required for the issuing of a visa.

To prevent refugees from coming upstairs to the consulate and thus avoid the risk of the staircase collapsing, he arranged for passports to be collected downstairs, and for people who had given in their passports to wait in the street so as not to obstruct the premises. At one point, Sousa Mendes even had a table from the consulate brought down and set up in the street.

David and Sylvain Bromberger, who were teenagers at the time, had fled Antwerp with their parents and reached Bayonne. 'I went upstairs with the crowd and gave all my family's passports in at the consulate,' David recalls. 'There were hundreds of people waiting,' says Sylvain, who stayed in the street. 'Then someone came down carrying a big bag full of passports. He started calling out names – but not ours. Then he opened a second bag and called out more names. Finally our passports emerged. I'll never forget that moment.'

Lissy Jarvik remembers seeing Sousa Mendes 'wearing a raincoat and a brown hat' and signing passports in the street. He also signed some at his hotel, in his car and anywhere else he could. His weapon was his pen, and he used it until the ink ran dry.

An increasingly panic-stricken Faria Machado asked Lisbon for instructions and told his superiors that, on Sousa Mendes's orders, he had issued visas without requesting a fee.

During the morning of 21 June, the ministry reacted. The secretary general, Luís de Sampaio, sent one of his trusted aides, Armando Lopo Simeão, on a special mission to Bayonne to see what was going on there. From there he would, if necessary, go on to Bordeaux to continue his investigations, then await instructions from the Portuguese ambassador in Spain, Pedro Teotónio Pereira, a member of Salazar's inner circle of friends.

The previous day, Pereira had written to the dictator to report on the Spanish government's dissatisfaction with the influx of refugees carrying Portuguese visas. Salazar, whose alliance with Franco was crucial, was furious. He never forgave Aristides de Sousa Mendes for having disrupted their happy relationship.

On 22 June, Pereira travelled to Irún and then to Bayonne, where he arrived during the night. He met Simeão, and together the two men drew up a text which laid down the basic elements of Portugal's new policy on the issuing of visas.

The text, which was tantamount to a death sentence on the thousands of refugees who had not yet managed to slip through the net, is chillingly clinical. First of all, it prohibits the issuing of visas to holders of so-called 'Nansen' passports – all those refugees, most of them Jews, who had left their country of origin and held temporary passports issued by the Society of Nations' refugee organization. There was one exception: such refugees would be issued with a visa if they could produce their boat ticket, thus proving that they were going to leave Europe – a more or less impossible condition except for a handful of wealthy people.

As regards other applicants, Pereira's absurd and cruel directives stipulated that nationals from only four countries would be able to obtain visas, and then only under certain conditions. While British and American citizens were to be admitted without any difficulty, French nationals had to be *gente limpa*. 'In the racist terminology that dated from the Portuguese Inquisition, that meant they were not Jews,' writes Rui Afonso.[2] As for the Belgians, only 'personalities' would be admitted. In the report he sent to Lisbon, Simeão encapsulated the callousness of his instructions in a single sentence: 'We wanted to keep out the mass of unworthy and socially undesirable people.'

What was Sousa Mendes up to as these unsavoury civil servants tried to cut off the escape route that was the only hope of salvation for thousands of people? He was signing visas in Hendaye. Caught between the Spanish, who were threatening to close the border, and the advancing Germans, the town had become an ultimate refuge. As the afternoon drew to a close, the refugees prepared to spend the night there as best they could. Afonso gives an extremely vivid account of the situation, based on the testimony of two Austrian refugees, Norbert and Heddy Gingold, and a Polish refugee, Nat Wyszkowski, who was a medical student:

Suddenly Sousa Mendes appeared in the middle of the square. According to Heddy Gingold, he was sur-rounded by a group of refugees. He continued issuing visas to those who asked him for them. [. . .] But what sort of visas were they? They consisted of a few words indicating that the holder was entitled to enter Portugal and carried Sousa Mendes's signature. He had certainly brought the consulate's rubber stamp with him. If refugees had passports, the visa featured on them. If they had only identity cards, he accepted those; and if they had neither, Sousa Mendes would make do with a sheet of paper, and sometimes even a piece of newspaper.[3]

'On 22 June, my father and mother crossed the Spanish border with a visa issued by Dr Mendes,' Steven Carol, another refugee, recalls. 'Since they were both Jewish and "stateless persons", my parents wouldn't have had much chance of escaping from the Germans!'

On 23 June, Salazar sent a telegram stripping Sousa Mendes of most of his attributions, and in particular the right to issue visas. By a strange coincidence, that was also the day when the decree cancelling de Gaulle's promotion to the rank of brigadier was published. So Sousa Mendes was in good company. Up until then, he had taken every possible liberty with his government's instructions, but he still retained a certain legality. From the moment he received Salazar's telegram, he was acting illegally.

But because he was in Hendaye it was not until later that he learned of Salazar's instructions. Sousa Mendes spun out his game of cat and mouse with his superiors for as long as possible. He realized he could still save some human lives, even though that was becoming increasingly difficult and the noose was tightening. For a fortnight, he divided his time between Bordeaux, Bayonne, Biarritz and Hendaye. On 23 June he was joined in Hendaye by Pereira, Simeão and Machado. Sousa Mendes did not have much to say to the Spanish ambassador.

'Orders must be obeyed,' Pereira said. 'Not if those orders are incompatible with any human feeling,' Sousa Mendes retorted. The four men returned to Bayonne. A few hours earlier, a girl refugee carrying a visa signed by Sousa Mendes had crossed the border. More than forty years later, pointing to the bridge she had crossed as a child, she described the scene in Andringa's documentary:

> That's the bridge we crossed. We got off the train on the French side, and then ran to catch the Spanish train on the other side. The bridge seemed enormous to me. On the far side, there was a passport control. We were terribly afraid the Spanish would force us to turn back towards Holland and put us into Hitler's hands.

On 24 June, Pereira authorized Sousa Mendes to return to Bordeaux. He did not do so, preferring to go back to the border. Salazar became increasingly restive: Sousa Mendes had to return to Lisbon. On 25 June, when the Franco-German armistice came into force and a day of national mourning was decreed, Salazar began to show increasingly visible signs of impatience: Lisbon had lost all trace of the Bordeaux consul.

But he was known to be in Bordeaux on 26 June, the day before the first convoys of German reconnaissance troops entered the city. The mayor of Bordeaux, Adrien Marquet, who was a minister of state in the new government, had the following 'Appeal to the population of Bordeaux' stuck up on the walls of the city:

> In our reverse of fortune, you have shown yourselves worthy of the city's traditions. You have been hospitable to the refugees, brave during the bombardments, and trusting in Marshal Pétain. Tomorrow as today, your instructions are: DISCIPLINE, ORDER, DIGNITY.

Simeão sent several telegrams from Bayonne to Lisbon. He seemed satisfied with what he had achieved:

> The consulate situation has been normalized. STOP. The French authorities are beginning to stop letting through people who got visas in Bordeaux. STOP. I shall only grant visas expressly authorized by Lisbon. STOP. Have put up on the consulate door the list of those who can obtain visas. STOP.

For the refugees who were still in Bordeaux, there was now no escape. A column of German vehicles was speeding towards the Basses-Pyrénées *département* in order to close off the Spanish border. Realizing they now no longer had any hope of getting out of France, many refugees started moving north. We shall never know how many of them ended up in concentration camps.

Sousa Mendes was back in Hendaye. Among the refugees who still managed to get across the border was the Bromberger family. 'I was quite unreasonably scared,' Sylvain Bromberger remembers. 'Spanish soldiers were stopping everyone and searching them. My father had heard that they would seize any valuables they found. Now in one of our suitcases there was our entire fortune – diamonds we had brought from Antwerp. We put down our luggage. A soldier came up and, pointing to that very suitcase, said: "I want to inspect this luggage." I then grabbed the suitcase and ran like mad. I managed to lose myself in the crowd. When we all met up again on the other side of the bridge, we looked back: the Germans had arrived.'

Others – many others – were not so lucky. Many refugees were turned back. Some preferred to commit suicide rather than fall into the hands of the Nazis.

Sousa Mendes then attempted the impossible. He remembered that when he drove back to Lisbon he used to cross the Franco–Spanish border at another point in order to avoid traffic jams on the bridge between Hendaye and Irún.

It was certainly worth a try. He asked the refugees with vehicles to follow his car. He drove slowly. The strange convoy turned up at the little border post. Fortunately the dumbfounded Spanish soldiers had no telephone, so had not yet received Madrid's new instructions that the border should be closed.

Although his clothes were crumpled, his shoes full of dust, his features drawn, and his hair dishevelled, Sousa Mendes still had considerable presence. He said to the Spanish soldiers: 'I'm the Portuguese consul. These people are with me. They all have regular visas, as you can check for yourselves, so would you be so kind as to let them through?'

Amazingly, they did precisely that. Once the convoy had crossed the border, Sousa Mendes was able to return to Bordeaux.

On 29 June, Marshal Pétain left Bordeaux for Clermont-Ferrand, before travelling on to Vichy. The only time he returned to Bordeaux was as a prisoner, stretched out on the back seat of a car, on 15 November 1945.

On 30 June, Colonel Kreschner, sporting an Iron Cross on his chest, was the first Wehrmacht officer to enter Bordeaux officially by the Pont de Pierre. The swastika was hoisted above the Germans' headquarters in Rue Vital-Carles. It was at that point that a man by the name of Lezer Karp decided to carry out the first act of heroism by the Resistance. Chédaille describes it as follows:

A German military band led by a towering drum major marched past crowds that feigned indifference. Suddenly a man who, on the contrary, had been staring intently at the intruders for some time darted out of the throng. With the quiet strength of those who act suicidally, he strode up to the huge Teutonic drum major at the head of the column of powerful, clattering and victorious troops, and raised his old man's stick against the German's drumstick. The soldier thrust it violently aside and swaggered on his way. His pathetic assailant, an elderly Jew crazed with hatred and desperate courage, was immediately arrested, court-martialled and shot.[4]

Simeão requested permission to return to Lisbon on 1 July. 'The consular situation is perfectly normal as regards passport visas,' he wrote, adding that there were rumours that German troops might push on to Gibraltar or Portugal. 'I was at the Spanish border when the German troops arrived,' he went on. 'I spoke to the military attaché, who seemed to have very kindly feelings towards our country and advised me to make the issuing of visas as difficult as possible.'

Back at Quai Louis-XVIII, Sousa Mendes was still trying to save those that could still be saved. He continued to receive refugees at his apartment. As he no longer had any official powers, he was forced to 'cheat'. Two Jews who had fled from Vienna, Mosco Galimir and his daughter

Marguerite, not only enjoyed his hospitality but were given fake Portuguese passports. 'Thanks to our Portuguese passports, we were protected by French authorities and not sent to concentration camp,' Marguerite wrote in 1966.

On 8 July, Aristides and Angelina Sousa Mendes returned to Portugal.

6. The Revenge of the Nonentities

On about 10 July 1940, Aristides and Angelina arrived in Cabanas de Viriato in a superb red Dodge Brother convertible. The consul still cut a fine figure, even if he had been exhausted by what he had gone through over the previous few weeks – and alarmed by the news that on 4 July Salazar had ordered the opening of disciplinary hearings against him.

Although he was aware he had taken liberties – to put it mildly – with the regulations, he felt at peace with his faith and his conscience. And he was not going to throw in the towel, especially not now that he was back at Passal, his home, where, as in the good old days, more than twenty people were awaiting him.

In addition to his children, who had one by one retreated to 'the palace', and a few cousins, there were Albert de Vleeschauwer's wife and children, as well as two of their friends. Everyone was enjoying a wonderful holiday. Father Van Rooy, a friend of the Vleeschauwers', insisted that one of the boys should serve Mass with him every morning. After that, the priest would summon all the children on to the big terrace for a gym lesson. He also taught them languages and tried to impose a minimum of discipline on the brood. It was not easy. On top of Sousa Mendes's twelve children, and one grandchild, Isabel's son Manuel, there were five Vleeschauwers, the youngest of whom was called Baudouin (which gave rise to a legend that the future king of Belgium had stayed at Cabanas). And then there were all the cousins.

The 'elder' children were extremely unruly and kept on playing practical jokes on the gardener, a clumsy hulk of a man whom they nicknamed 'Stalin', and who spent his whole time chasing them out of the garden because they trampled on his flowers. Aristides, the eldest son, kept increasingly out of things. José, who had come from Bordeaux, was taunted by his brothers because of his 'pro-Salazar' leanings. 'Go and put on your green shirt [the uniform of the party's youth section],' they chanted. As Clotilde and Isabel were already married, it was the three 'students' – Geraldo, Pedro Nuno and Sebastião – who ruled the roost.

Pedro Nuno was deeply in love with his beautiful cousin Maria Adelaide, who was César's daughter. They were both conceived in Brazil and born on almost the same day. Pedro Nuno often went to see her at César's house in Mangualde. He would don his best clothes and the two-tone shoes of which he was so proud. Indeed he was so proud of them that Sebastião once played a practical joke of the poorest taste on him: he urinated into them.

Several times a week the jolly little group would organize memorable picnics in the mountains. The husband of one of Aristides's nieces, a young jurist from Cape Verde, drove the 'coach'. Ludovic de Vleeschauwer, who was fourteen at the time, remembers the excursions well: 'You should have seen us on those bumpy little roads – it was no joke! We'd take a dip in little mountain streams, eat bread, cheese and quince paste, and drink local wine.'

In the evening, they made music in the drawing-room or on the terrace, which was decorated with multicoloured Chinese lanterns. The inhabitants of Cabanas looked on spellbound as they all danced. 'There were almost thirty of us at table, and we were waited on by the servants,' remembers Elsa de Vleeschauwer, who was very young at the time. The war certainly seemed very remote.

What sort of state was Aristides in when he returned to Cabanas? Ludovic de Vleeschauwer remembers him as being 'dignified, calm, smiling and very indulgent with the children'. Today Sebastião confirms that his father, as often happens in large families, was much stricter with his elder brothers than he was with him. 'Aristides was quite portly, and spoke in a very calm voice. He was always very amiable,' Ludovic de Vleeschauwer recalls, 'whereas Angelina seemed extremely weary. I don't remember her ever giving a single order in the house.' His sister, Elsa, remembers Aristides as a 'warm and jovial man – though it's true that when one is a child one has an amazing ability not to notice adults' worries'.

Sousa Mendes had indeed much to worry about. He did not stay long in Cabanas, as his future hung in the balance in Lisbon. He and Angelina settled in the capital, at 170 Rua Rodrigues Sampaio, near Avenida da Liberdade.

Aristides was unfamiliar with Lisbon and its intrigues. He had always only passed through the capital on his way from one posting to another, without being able to set up a real network of friendships and contacts. Nor was he really aware of the nature of the Salazar regime.

In the summer of 1940, Lisbon was in a state of effervescence. Tens of thousands of refugees had settled there. Douglas Wheeler quotes a description of the city by Dusko Popov, one of Britain's top double agents:

> In 1940, Lisbon was a very special universe, a tiny enclave of neutrality, where all sides in the war brushed shoulders. It was filled with refugees of all descriptions and all nations. Some were wealthy beyond measure, and they squandered their money like [*sic*] there was no tomorrow, as there might not have been. Some were impoverished to the point where they would sell anything, which usually meant themselves.[1]

Famous refugees included the writer Arthur Koestler, the Duke and Duchess of Windsor, the French playwright Jean Giraudoux, and the novelist Erich Maria Remarque.

The war was at Portugal's door, and everyone talked about it without realizing the scale of the catastrophe. But the main talking point in Lisbon in the summer of 1940 was the Exhibition of the Portuguese World, which was inaugurated with much pomp and circumstance by Salazar in June 1940. It was intended to be a great nationalist event, but also a symbol of peace. As one of the captions in Mariana Tavares Dias's remarkable book of photographs[2] puts it: 'A show conceived on the scale of the Portuguese people's pride and fears of the time, in the heyday of a regime that would never again enjoy such an ideal state of isolation.'

Above the caption is a photograph of Salazar and 'his' president of the republic, Carmona, seated in wicker chairs and conversing. The dictator is dressed entirely in black and wearing his celebrated lace-up black boots; his black hat is on his lap. Another photograph, taken on the day when the exhibition was inaugurated, shows Salazar surrounded by some of his ministers, all of them wearing black hats.

Yves Léonard well describes 'the sometimes surprising mixtures emblematically illustrated by the Exhibition of the Portuguese World, which combined modernistic approaches – and even futuristic experiments such as the pavilions designed by Cristino da Silva – with typically traditional village houses, Manoeline art, armillary spheres and coats of arms that go to make up an "eight-century-old" national identity'.[3]

If Sousa Mendes did not know Lisbon very well, he was even less familiar with Salazar and the regime he had set up.

When he left Bordeaux, he seemed convinced he would be able to go and see Salazar and explain to him why, in the name of Christian ethics which he believed they shared, he had saved so many people. He assumed that he would be able to tell him that he had also saved the honour of his country, that this would one day serve Portugal's cause, and that he would be able to appeal not only to his Christian sentiments and his generosity, but to his intelligence and what he believed to be his vision of the world.

He wrote to Salazar: 'Aware as I am of having carried out my duty to my country and of not having shown myself unworthy of Your Excellency's esteem, I would be most grateful if you would be so kind as to grant me an audience. Yours faithfully, Aristides de Sousa Mendes.'

The dictator with the lace-up boots never granted Sousa Mendes an audience. He did everything in his power to crush him. Sousa Mendes had not grasped the essential trait of his former fellow student at Coimbra University: a fanatical, immoderate and pathological love of law and order. Salazar did not care about the thousands of people Sousa Mendes had saved or his invocations of the Christian faith. They were nothing compared to the really serious crime of not having obeyed a government directive. Never – neither in 1940, nor in 1945, nor in 1950 – did Salazar grasp the ethical and political significance of Sousa Mendes's action. He could interpret it only as disobedience. And disobedience was a punishable offence.

Francisco de Paula Brito Júnior, head of the department of economic affairs in the Foreign Ministry, was entrusted with the task of drawing up the bill of indictment for the Sousa Mendes hearings. On 26 June Pedro Lemos, Count Tovar, director general of political and consular affairs, had already formulated a series of complaints about the Bordeaux consul's behaviour. Salazar had also initiated his own investigations. He sent telegrams to several people asking them to say what had happened and indicate the precise nature of the orders given to Sousa Mendes.

Brito based his inquiry mainly on the declarations of three witnesses: Captain Agostinho Lourenço, who was head of the public security department, Armando Lopo Simeão, Salazar's special envoy in Bayonne, and Pedro Teotónio Pereira, the Portuguese ambassador in Madrid.

Lourenço, who had often travelled to the Spanish–Portuguese border in an attempt to control the influx of refugees, confirmed that many of them had visas issued by the Bordeaux consulate. He also insisted on the fact that most of the refugees should never have entered Portugal in the first place, since they belonged to the categories of 'banned' people specified in Circular 14.

Lourenço also stressed the 'mistakes' that Sousa Mendes had made before matters came to a head in June, and notably the visas and fake passport issued to the Miny couple, and the assistance given to Wiznitzer and Dr Laporte.

The second witness for the prosecution, Simeão, emphasized the psychological state in which he found Sousa Mendes. Simeão explained that, 'although he was not insane' and was 'in perfect possession of his faculties', he presented 'serious signs of stubbornness'. Simeão said that, despite warnings 'about the gravity of his attitude' which he had repeatedly addressed to Sousa Mendes, the latter 'kept on retorting that to refuse all those poor people visas constituted an effort that was quite beyond his capabilities'.

Pereira's evidence was the most damning for Sousa Mendes. First of all, he confirmed that in the course of his inquiries at the Irún border he too had noted that most of the refugees' visas had been issued by the Bordeaux consulate. He specified that Sousa Mendes had ordered the consul in Bayonne to go on issuing visas.

In describing how he had met Sousa Mendes at the Franco-Spanish border, Pereira wanted to prove that the accused had gone out of his mind: 'I asked him to explain the situation to me. [. . .] From what he told me, and to judge from his dishevelled appearance, I got the impression of a deeply perturbed man who was not in his normal state.'

'Sousa Mendes's attitude suggested such a degree of disturbance that I hastened to draw it to the attention of the Spanish authorities,' Pereira went on. 'And I asked them to regard any visas that had already been issued as invalid. There was not the slightest doubt in my mind when I told the Spanish authorities that the consul had taken leave of his senses.'

Given what he said at the time, one can feel nothing but disgust on reading Pereira's version of events in his *Memórias* (1973).[4]

On June 20, I took the decision to go to the French border. I had received news that a multitude of fugitives of various nationalities had congregated at the Pyrenees border and, in fear of their lives, were trying to continue on their way as far as Portugal.

For two or three days, I made the difficult journey between Hendaye and Bayonne, forcing the Spanish authorities to respect the Portuguese visas and trying to help all those poor people by every means at my disposal.

On 2 August, Brito of the Foreign Office handed over to Sousa Mendes the bill of indictment he had drawn up. It contained fifteen charges:

1. The issuing of visas to Arnold Wiznitzer and his family before even receiving Lisbon's reply;

2. The issuing under similar circumstances of visas to Professor Laporte;

3. The violation of Circular 14 by issuing visas to three Polish nationals;

4. The request made to British nationals that they should contribute to a Portuguese charity before being granted visas;

5. The order given to the consul in Bayonne to issue visas to all those who asked for them, 'with the claim that it was necessary to save all these people';

6. The exercise of his functions in a chancellery that was not his own, and the order given to the consul in Bayonne to distribute visas free of charge;

7. The permission given by telephone to the consul in Toulouse that he could issue visas;

8. The reply to Armando Simeão, who had insisted on the seriousness of his misconduct: 'To refuse all those poor people visas constituted an effort that was quite beyond his capabilities';

9. The creation of a situation that was dishonourable for Portugal vis-à-vis the Spanish and German authorities;

10. The fact that the head of the intelligence service had been able to verify that most of the aliens wishing to enter Portugal had had their documents signed by the defendant;

11. The presence among these aliens of people of many nationalities to whom it was forbidden to grant a visa;

12. The stamping of visas on documents that were not even passports;

13. The entry into Portugal of two Luxembourg nationals, Paul Miny and Maria da Conceição Miny, with Portuguese passports;

14. The falsification of the family ties that existed between Paul and Maria Miny;

15. The defendant's request to the Miny couple that they

should return the contentious passport to him after their entry into Portugal.

Sousa Mendes was given ten days in which to prepare his defence. He called three witnesses. The first of these was Francisco Calheiros e Meneses, the Portuguese ambassador in Brussels who had retreated to Bordeaux as the Germans advanced. He did not deny the acts with which Sousa Mendes was charged, but insisted in his written statement on the tragic nature of the events facing the defendant, his great physical fatigue and his moral distress, all of which he regarded as extenuating circumstances.

'A civil servant must not be humane when it is a question of obeying orders,' Meneses wrote, 'but not everyone has the same moral resilience to face the situations that Aristides de Sousa Mendes experienced. Others might have shown themselves to be intellectually, physically and morally stronger and thus resisted the vehement and anguished pleas of those who were suffering.' Brito concluded: 'The witness believes that the consul in Bordeaux allowed himself to be dominated, as were many others, by the horror of the tragedy he witnessed.'

The two other witnesses called by the defence, the consular inspector Agapito Pedroso Rodrigues and the consul Agnelo Lopes da Cunha Pessoa, were not present at the time of the events and stressed Sousa Mendes's moral and professional integrity. 'I have known him for almost thirty years,' said Pessoa, 'and I have never learnt of anything that could possibly reflect badly on his moral qualities.'

On 12 August Sousa Mendes presented his defence, a document of twenty pages to which he appended an article headlined 'Portugal has always been Christian' in the daily newspaper *Diário de Notícias*, which paid tribute to the hospitality the country had extended to refugees.

The paper quoted in particular a statement by the Dutch ambassador in Lisbon which congratulated Portugal for the hospitality, 'during this dramatic period in the history of Europe', that it had granted foreigners 'who were seeking refuge on [our] territory from the dangers of the time'. The newspaper went on: 'Our hospitality has no colour, nor is it guided by any other feeling than the human virtue of solidarity in the face of helpless or innocent distress, or a disinterested appeal.'

Diário de Notícias concluded as follows: 'In one of the pavilions [at the Exhibition of the Portuguese World] there is a cross with the following inscription: "Portugal has always been Christian". It is the image of an essentially generous trait that is deeply rooted in our soul.'

Sousa Mendes appended to his dossier a letter written in French from the writer Gisèle Quittner Allotini: 'I would like to make a point of telling you how deeply admired you are in all the foreign countries where you have served as consul. You are the best advertisement for Portugal and a credit to your country. All those who have known you praise your courage, your kind-heartedness and your gentlemanly spirit, adding that if the Portuguese are like consul general Mendes they must be a people of knights and heroes.'

In his defence, Sousa Mendes took up Brito's fifteen accusations one by one.

Regarding Arnold Wiznitzer's visa, Sousa Mendes wrote: 'He was going to be interned in a concentration camp, which would have deprived his wife and family of his support [. . .]. I considered that it was a duty of basic humanity to spare him such an ordeal.'

As for the help he gave Dr Laporte, he wrote: 'He had excellent references, and I had already asked the ministry for an authorization a month earlier. I could see no reason why the ministry should refuse him that visa. The fact that the authorities took no steps to stop him passing through Lisbon seems to confirm that my decision was correct.'

Sousa Mendes then described as 'groundless' the accusation by the British embassy in Lisbon that he had worked outside normal hours and requested extra fees for the issue of visas. He explained that he had 'never granted visas outside working hours', but that the consulate's official opening hours had become very long. 'The service was open from 9a.m., and very often a little before then, and for a period of several weeks continued until 1 or 2a.m.'

As for the accusation that extra fees had been charged, it must have resulted from a 'misunderstanding on the part of the informer at the British embassy'. 'In accordance with the consular tariffs, I was entitled to receive a personal indemnity for each service rendered outside official hours, and yet I never asked for one.' 'There was one exception, however,' he added, 'on a Sunday, when I deemed it appropriate to ask Robert Rothschild, who refused to wait until the next day, for that indemnity.'

'It would be absurd to suppose that I could have demanded contributions to Portuguese charities,' he went on, 'and there is no justification for saying that that happened in my consulate.' Regarding the whole series of accusations formulated by the British embassy, Sousa Mendes wondered whether they may not have originated from an English-woman who was fed up with waiting for her visa at the Portuguese consulate and in a fit of bad temper had an argument with the staff and announced she would be lodging a complaint.

In reply to points 5 and 6 of the bill of indictment, Sousa Mendes explained that he had gone to Bayonne in response to a request by consul Machado: 'As there was a veritable state of panic throughout south-west France, which mounted steadily as news of the French troops' retreat came through, I thought it was my strict duty in the circumstances to go and help my Bayonne colleague personally.

'With thousands of people crowding in front of the consul-ate and in the streets of the town, I suggested to my colleague Machado that the only solution would be to grant everyone visas. I also knew that it was materially impossible to guaran-tee the collection of fees in full, and that it would always be possible to do that at the Portuguese border.'

Sousa Mendes then stated that Faria Machado had agreed to his suggestion in the presence of the Portuguese ambassador in Brussels, Calheiros e Meneses.

'My aim was first and foremost humanitarian,' he wrote. 'Lives had to be saved, and families prevented from being split up. I also thought of the fate that would be in store for those people were they to fall into the hands of the enemy. Many of them were Jews who had already been hounded and who were trying to escape from the horror of further persecution. There was also an incalculable number of women from all the invaded countries who wanted to avoid finding themselves at the mercy of the Teutons' brutal sex drive, and children who had witnessed their parents' suffering.

'I have been privy to countless suicides and other acts of desperation,' he went on, before pointing out that if he had authorized the consul in Toulouse to issue visas himself it was because it was impossible for all the refugees to go to Bordeaux or Bayonne.

As for the question of dishonouring Portugal, Sousa Mendes felt it was 'obvious' that his attitude may have been a little 'strange'. 'But it should be remembered that everything was strange at that time, and that my action can be usefully appraised only by someone with a precise knowledge of the context and what was going on.

'I deeply regret that this impression of dishonour should have germinated in some people's minds,' he declared, while at the same time asking why he had been accused of having dishonoured his country in the eyes of German authorities who were not even in Bordeaux at the time that the events in question occurred. He added that the French authorities had understood what was going on perfectly well, when they stopped issuing exit visas two days before the arrival of German troops.

Sousa Mendes concluded his remarks on 'dishonour' by saying that when he left Bayonne he was applauded by hundreds of people, and through him it was Portugal that was being honoured.

As for the Miny couple, Sousa Mendes simply stated that in this case too he had acted on humanitarian grounds.

He concluded by explaining that he had first and foremost sought to honour the task that was incumbent upon him to defend Portugal's good name, that many leading figures from foreign countries had turned to him for help, and that all had expressed their gratitude not only to him, but to Portugal, the only country in Europe to welcome so many people in a terrible predicament.

'It may be,' he concluded, 'that I made mistakes, but if I did so it was not on purpose, for I have always acted according to my conscience. I was guided solely by a sense of duty, fully aware as I was of my responsibilities.'

On 29 August, Brito presented his report to the disciplinary council: Aristides de Sousa Mendes was accused of disobedience, premeditation, reoffending and multiple offences.

Brito attached great importance to the fact that Sousa Mendes had issued passports to the Miny couple, and accused him of having 'caused a situation that reflected very badly on Portugal in the eyes of the Spanish authorities and German occupying forces'.

He repeated that the head of the political and state security police had remarked that most of the aliens who had turned up at the Portuguese border held visas issued by the defendant, and that they included a large number of citizens from countries which, according to the ministry's instructions, did not entitle them to receive visas. Many visas, he added, had been stamped on ordinary identity cards. But Brito believed that Sousa Mendes should benefit from extenuating circumstances and therefore suggested that his punishment should consist of a suspension from active service for a period of one to six months.

His report was passed on to his hierarchical superior, Count Tovar, who on 1 October was appointed judge advocate of the hearings against Sousa Mendes. He handed down his verdict on 19 October. It was harsher than the one suggested by Brito. Tovar ruled out any extenuating circumstances, in view of the fact that Sousa Mendes had reoffended. He also criticized him because, far from regretting his action, he had delighted in it. Regarding him as unsuitable to run a consulate, he advised that Sousa Mendes should be demoted to the rank below that of consul. On 29

October, his report was approved by the disciplinary council.

The verdict was harsh and outrageously unfair. But it would have enabled Sousa Mendes to continue working and eventually to consider embarking on a new career. However, there was another element in the equation: Salazar, whose vindictiveness was to manifest itself on the following day, 30 October 1940. The dictator, flouting the administrative regulations then in force, which prohibited double sentencing, ruled not only that Sousa Mendes should withdraw from active service for one year, on half pay, but that when that year had elapsed he should be forced to retire. 'Whereas Tovar had in fact tried to save Sousa Mendes by demoting him, Salazar condemned him to financial ruin,' says Calvet de Magalhães, who served as a minister under Salazar.

Salazar placed seals on the dossier, in rather the same way as a stone is traditionally placed on a dried-up well. He wanted to hear no more of Aristides de Sousa Mendes.

7. 'We are all refugees'

Forced to retire at the age of fifty-five and out of a job, Aristides de Sousa Mendes still had virtually a whole family to feed. He faced up to the challenge. Another event had taken place, which filled him with both joy and anxiety: the birth on 19 October, at the Alfredo da Costa maternity hospital in Lisbon, of Marie-Rose, the daughter that Andrée Cibial had conceived with him in Bordeaux. The child was placed in the charge of her uncle and aunt in Ribérac.

Convinced that he had acted honourably by issuing visas, Sousa Mendes continued to justify himself to the Portuguese authorities. Clearly he had not yet measured the degree to which Salazar could be vindictive and callous.

At about the same time another diplomat, who believed he was in favour with the authorities, was also on the receiving end of Salazar's wrath. He was the Portuguese ambassador in Berlin and wanted to return to Lisbon for family reasons. Salazar ordered him to remain at his post. In the belief that he would be able to sway the prime minister, the diplomat

15. The three eldest Sousa Mendes sons, Aristides,
Manuel and José, *c.* 1933

16. Four Sousa Mendes daughters with cousins in Louvain in 1932: Joana (*far left*), Clotilde (*fourth from left*), Isabel (*third from right*) and Teresinha (*far right*). Raquel was still an infant. Their brother Luís Filipe is half hidden in the bush on the left

17. The nine Sousa Mendes sons in Louvain in 1932: (*back row from left*) Manuel, Aristides, Geraldo and José; (*in the front from left*) Sebastião, Pedro Nuno, Luís Filipe, Carlos, João Paulo

18. Aristides de Sousa Mendes at an official function in Antwerp, *c.* 1934

19. The wedding of Clotilde de Sousa Mendes and Silvério Moncada Alpoim de Sousa Mendes in 1940

20. Refugees crossing the Pont de Pierre in Bordeaux in June 1940. Etching by Charles Philippe

21. Refugees in front of Bordeaux City Hall in 1940

Nous Aristides de Sousa Mendes *Consul de la République Portugaise à Bordeaux*

N° **5 5**

SIGNALEMENT

âge 36 ans

taille

les

cheveux

sourcils

yeux

barbe

menton

SIGNES PARTICULIERS

Signature du porteur,

da Conceicão les de Castro

Faisons savoir à tous ceux qui verront le présent passeport que la citoyen portugais M. da Conceição Teles e C A S T R O M I N Y -------------------- , âgé de 36 ans, né à Lisboa (Portugal) de profession Sans fil de Dr.Ricardo Teles de Castro et de Madame A. Lucia de Taveres de Castro dont signalement et signature en marge, part de cette ville à desti- nation de -:- PORTUGAL via ESPAGNE et retour en FRANCE accompagné de son Paul agê de 19 ans. -----------

Prions, en conséquence, toutes les autorités civiles ou militaires auxquelles ce passeport sera présenté, de laisser passer librement le porteur et de lui donner tout aide et protection en cas de besoin pour son voyage.

Le présent passeport est personnel et valable pour un an.

Consulat de Portugal à Bordeaux, le 30 mai 19 40

Le Consul,

Aristides de Sousa Mendes

Passaporte não é válido para a Rússia, nem pode noste por outro Consulado qualquer visto que lhe dê validade para pais.

Présent passeport n'est pas valable pour la Russie, nul visa y par un autre Consulat ne saurait lui conférer validité pour ce pays.

Présent passport is not valid for Russia. Any visa for the Country shall not be granted by another Consulate.

Pass hat keine Geltung

Pagou ao câmbio de 1,60 a quantia de Frs: 160,00 segundo o número 9.C da tabela, ficando esta importância lançada no livro da re- ceita sob o número 1.175 Consulado de Portugal em Bordéus, aos Maio 40

22. Visa issued by Aristides de Sousa Mendes in May 1940

23 The Prime Minister of Portugal, Dr António de Oliveira Salazar, at a meeting of the Portuguese Legion in Lisbon, 11 March 1938. He is giving his Fascist-style salute

24. Refugees in front of the Gare Saint-Jean in Bordeaux in 1940

26. The last photograph of Aristides de Sousa Mendes, taken in Lisbon a few days before his death

25. Andrée Cibial

27. Passal, once the home of the Sousa Mendes family, in about 1995

28. Rabbi Chaim Kruger, Israeli consul general Michael Arnon and João Paulo de Sousa Mendes (John Paul Abranches) at a ceremony in 1967 when Aristides de Sousa Mendes was posthumously declared 'a Righteous Gentile' by the Yad Vashem Holocaust Remembrance Authority

29. A stela placed in a forest in Israel which was planted to commemorate the heroism of Aristides de Sousa Mendes. On it is inscribed: 'Forest in memory of Dr Aristides de Sousa Mendes, a Righteous Gentile. Portuguese Consul General at Bordeaux in 1940. Against the orders of his government he issued visas to 10,000 Jews saving them from certain death. He was dismissed, disgraced and died in poverty. June 1994.'

arrived in Lisbon. He was shown into the office of Salazar's secretary, who announced him: 'Prime Minister, the Portuguese ambassador in Berlin is here.' 'You are mistaken – our ambassador is not in Lisbon, he is in Berlin.' And that was that: the ambassador never saw Salazar and never obtained any other posting abroad.

On 28 November Sousa Mendes, with the help of Adelino da Palma Carlos, a lawyer who had already brushed with the regime's political police, prepared an appeal before the administrative tribunal. He insisted chiefly on the fact that his rights had not been taken into account during the disciplinary hearing. He also stressed the confusion of the arguments put forward by the various people responsible for the hearing and the divergence between the proposed punishment and that actually enforced. Repeating arguments he had already put forward, he explained why he had issued visas.

With regard to Arnold Wiznitzer, Sousa Mendes clearly believed in what he was saying when he wrote: 'If he had not had a visa, the professor would have been interned in a concentration camp.' He added, somewhat naïvely: 'If, on the other hand, the professor could come to Portugal, he would study here in a calmer and safer environment [. . .]. A university professor can in no way be regarded as undesirable.'

Pointing out that Dr Laporte had produced the 'best references' from the French authorities, and that exceptional circumstances had justified his action in favour of the Miny couple, Sousa Mendes came to his main point: they were not normal times. 'In September 1939, war was declared between France and Germany,' he went on. Referring to 'the flight of all those who, through their own experience or by tradition, were familiar with what the German occupation meant' and 'a period that could not be described to those who did not experience it', he was insistent that 'this is what cannot be forgotten'.

In his view, there was one element – a moral element – that was missing if he was to be deemed to have committed an offence. He asked the president of the tribunal to take into consideration 'the powerful imperatives of human solidarity' that lay behind his action, and concluded that the quashing of the judgment against him would be 'an act of pure justice'.

As he waited for the administrative tribunal to come to its decision, Sousa Mendes, who was in an increasingly disastrous financial situation, sent another telegram to Salazar in December 1940. He mentioned his 'absolute need of funds' in order to be able to provide for the needs of his family, 'one of the largest in Portugal', and begged 'His Excellency to be so good as to order as urgently as possible that the sums to which [he] was entitled should be paid [to him]'.

But answer came there none. The Jewish community in Lisbon granted Sousa Mendes a monthly allowance and let him eat at its soup kitchen with his children. Isaac Bitton, then a young man, helped his aunt in the kitchen. Clearly moved, he described the scene in Diana Andringa's television documentary: 'One day I heard a voice behind me speaking perfect Portuguese. I turned round and saw a man wearing a black suit and a diplomat's hat, accompanied by his wife and several children. Impressed by his presence, I went up to him and told him that next to the dining-room for refugees there was another room, on the left, for the Portuguese. He looked at me with a strange smile and said in a very calm voice: "You know, we are all refugees."

On 19 June 1941, Sousa Mendes received yet another piece of bad news: the administrative tribunal had turned down his appeal. Its main reason for doing so was that 'a civil servant is not competent to question orders which he must obey'. And yet there was ample justification: by the year 1942, Europe had been engulfed in a bloody, lethal and inhuman tragedy. The first convoys of Jews had left from Drancy, near Paris, for Auschwitz. Every single deportee proved that those who did not obey were right. The Final Solution had got under way, and in Lisbon a man was being castigated for having issued visas outside office hours.

Life was getting more and more difficult for Sousa Mendes. He was forced to take out more and more mortgages on Passal. Pedro Nuno and Maria Adelaide's wedding in June 1942 was probably the last family celebration.

In Lisbon, their servant Fernanda, who was still called by her nickname, the '*petiza*' (young girl), often went to fetch food for Aristides and Angelina from the Jewish community's soup kitchen. Aristides used up all his energies making point-

less appeals to the authorities. At the Foreign Ministry building – the Palácio das Necessidades he entered so proudly in
1910 – he was kept waiting like an intruder. 'One evening,
the consul came home after a day of waiting at the ministry,'
Fernanda told *Expresso*.[1] He put down his hat and, before
even sitting down, kept on repeating: 'No! That just isn't
done, that just isn't done!'

On another occasion, when Fernanda's husband was
accompanying Sousa Mendes to the doctor's, they passed a
car containing a leading member of the regime who knew
Sousa Mendes well. 'He pretended not to see him, even
though the consul had paid his respects very politely,' Fernanda said.

Later, at Cabanas de Viriato, Sousa Mendes told Fernanda's
mother, Claudina, how terribly sorry he was 'not to have
been able to give the *petiza* the future she deserved'. As
Fernanda graciously put it later on: 'Even if there was bitterness, the past with Aristides de Sousa Mendes was much
better than any other future.'

In June 1943, Carlos 'the archbishop' and Sebastião 'the
American' enlisted in the American army in Europe. They
were both born in Berkeley, in 1920 and 1923 respectively,
and later took American nationality. They were sent to
Britain. Carlos remained in London, then went to Paris,
while Sebastião was parachuted over Normandy on D-Day
– not far from Avranches.

Salazar continued to finesse with the Axis powers and

the Allies. In 1943 Churchill said he felt that Salazar was 'intolerable'. Salazar's great dream was to separate Britain from the Soviet Union and work for a compromise peace between London and Berlin.

'Without being totally convinced that Germany would triumph, Salazar ruled out an eventual British victory,' writes Yves Léonard.[2] 'It was a fact that the Germans, whose image and popularity in Lisbon had improved distinctly since the beginning of the war, exploited the anti-communism of the Salazar regime all the more adroitly because they knew they could rely on valuable support and co-operation within the Portuguese government and the corridors of power.'

In this connection, Léonard quotes an edifying entry in Joseph Goebbels's diary for 6 March 1943:[3]

> Salazar delivered an exceptionally sharp anti-Bolshevik speech, which, however, has not been released for general use. He delivered it to a small group. It sufficed, however, to enable us to conclude that as long as Salazar is in power in Portugal, nothing really hostile to us will be done.

While the Nazis were stepping up the pace of extermination in the concentration camps, the military situation was becoming increasingly difficult for them. On 30 April 1945, Hitler committed suicide. Salazar was the only leader, apart from the Irish president Eamon de Valera, who sent a telegram of condolences; and for two days the flags were half-masted in Lisbon. That did not prevent Salazar, when he addressed parliament on 8 May, from announcing: 'We bless peace, we bless victory.'

That day, there was enormous public rejoicing in the capital. 'Praça do Rossio was teeming with people, and they were clearly expecting something,' wrote Mário Soares.[4] 'There was a huge crowd. Thousands and thousands of people were chanting "Victory, victory" [. . .]. There were cries of "Down with fascism! Freedom for all political prisoners!" [. . .] We handed in very explicit messages to the ambassadors of the Allies. They were embarrassed, answered us with purely token thanks and gave our cheering a cool reception. Perhaps they already knew they were going to betray us.'

Like so many of his compatriots, Sousa Mendes believed that change was possible in Portugal. Although he suffered a stroke in May 1945, he kept on fighting. Salazar's 'Peace speech' of 16 May shocked him particularly, above all when the dictator declared: 'As regards the refugees, we did our duty, though it is a pity we could not do more.' Aristides, such a calm and benign man most of the time, went into a fit of rage.

Salazar had conjured everything away – Circular 14, all the people the Portuguese authorities wanted to allow the Nazis to deport, the bowing and scraping before the Germans, who at all costs must not be upset, Sousa Mendes's trial for having disobeyed inhuman orders, and his demotion.

Sebastião, after returning to London, visited his parents in Lisbon. 'I met them in the street, in front of their home,' he remembers. 'It was a very emotional occasion for all three of us, as they weren't expecting me, and I had not been able to give them any news for reasons of military security. I thought they had both aged a great deal and looked very tired. My father, who had been ill, had difficulty in walking.'

Sebastião was never to see his parents again, since he did not return to Portugal until 1967. When he took leave of them, he made a promise to his father. 'I shall tell the whole world what you did in Bordeaux.' With Carlos, he took an American troop ship from Le Havre. He soon found work in a bank.

He also wrote his own version of his father's exploits. *Flight through Hell*,[5] which he finished writing in 1949 and signed Michael d'Avranches – 'a pseudonym, so it would look as though I had myself been a refugee' – was the first written work devoted to the life of Aristides de Sousa Mendes.

At the end of 1945, Sousa Mendes was still looking for a job. Although he was reinstated by the association of barristers in 1941, he had still not actually practised. Indeed, he was eventually excluded from the association for not paying his membership fees. In September, and again in November, César, who had been appointed ambassador to Mexico, wrote to Salazar to inform him of his twin brother's state of health and to request his rehabilitation.

Alluding to Salazar's speech on 16 May, César wrote in September: 'There was a passage in Your Excellency's speech which left a great impression on me, and in which you referred to the reception given to the refugees and the many other manifestations of human solidarity and charity on the part of the Portuguese people. Your Excellency no doubt remembers that my brother Aristides facilitated the entry of the fugitives into Portugal. He did so, inspired exclusively by the sentiments which so fully and so nobly characterize the Portuguese soul. In my capacity as his twin brother, I ask Your Excellency to make his rehabilitation possible.'

César described Aristides's 'deep depression' and illnesses. 'I implore Your Excellency not to let him die,' he went on. It is easy to imagine how difficult it was for him to write those words.

César was to drain the bitter cup to the dregs. 'Pardon me, Your Excellency, if I offend you in any way, but I am a very devoted brother and it would be wrong of me not to employ all the methods at my disposal to save his honour and very probably his life. Might not Your Excellency, head of an outstandingly Christian government, grant clemency to my brother, keeping in mind all the suffering he has experienced and is still experiencing?'

After getting no reply, César had another try in November, shortly after learning that Salazar had decided to dissolve the Chamber of Deputies, call a new election and grant an amnesty. 'I implore the forgiveness of Your Excellency,' he

wrote. 'I beg you to pardon this tortured prayer. My brother
has always been a generous and good man, and has helped
to save countless lives. Your Excellency has just announced
a sufficiently wide-ranging amnesty [. . .]. Your Excellency
would be carrying out an act of sublime generosity that
would greatly ennoble him if he did not forget to include
my brother in his clemency.'

In November, Aristides de Sousa Mendes and his sons Aristides, José, Geraldo and Pedro Nuno signed a petition put
out by the new Movement of Democratic Unity (MUD),
which campaigned chiefly in favour of free elections. Despite
promises from the authorities, the lists of the movement's
members and sympathizers fell into the hands of the political
police, which summoned the Sousa Mendes family. The
press was once again gagged, and the opposition preferred to
abstain at the November poll.

Salazar founded the essence of his election campaign on
his policy of neutrality during the war. One of his election
posters read as follows: 'Portuguese women! You can thank
Salazar for the fact that your husbands, brothers and sons are
alive, that they did not set off for the battlefield. You can
thank Salazar for the fact that your fiancés did not die in a
foreign land after being put to the fire and the sword, and
that you can start a happy and trouble-free home and family!'

The November election, which was marked by a very
high abstention rate, enabled Salazar to strengthen his grip

on power. The Western countries left Portugal to its own devices. With the help of the Cold War, Salazar used his anti-communism as a way of joining the Western camp. The dictator also admirably exploited his country's 'hospitality' towards the refugees, and particularly the Jews, as a way of pleading his case in Washington, London and Paris.

The general feeling in those capitals was that a dictator who had saved so many people could not be as bad as all that. Little did people know that the man who had taken so many risks to help the refugees to escape had been condemned by his superiors and had failed to obtain a straightforward rehabilitation. It was probably due to a lack of information. But there was also an unwillingness to listen to a man who was screaming into the wind.

In December 1945, Sousa Mendes wrote to the president of the National Assembly. He tried a more direct line of attack, claiming that Circular 14 was quite simply unconstitutional. What he had done, he said, was give visas 'to thousands of people of Jewish belief, to nationals from all the invaded countries, who had already been persecuted in Germany and other countries. I believed I should not obey the ban on giving them visas, because I saw it as contradicting Article 8 of the constitution which guarantees the freedom and inviolability of beliefs by making it illegal for anyone to be persecuted because of those beliefs, or to be forced to reveal their religion.'

Now observance of the ministry's instructions involved

asking people to state their religion, meaning they might subsequently be refused a visa. Sousa Mendes countered the arguments of those who claimed that the constitution applied to the Portuguese and not to aliens: 'We are talking not about the right of aliens, but about a duty of Portuguese civil servants who may not – either in Portugal or in consulates, which are also Portuguese territory – question anyone about their religion without contradicting the principles of the constitution.' Sousa Mendes concluded by expressing the hope that the National Assembly, 'accomplishing its noble function of ensuring that the law is carried out', would decide to quash the penalty that had been inflicted on him.

The former consul went further. He pointed out that, because of the war in Europe, he had not wished to publicize the attitude of other civil servants who had obeyed unconstitutional orders. He felt, moreover, that those civil servants, 'in so far as they adopted an attitude that could be interpreted as collaboration with Hitler's persecution of the Jews, could signal the end of the policy of neutrality adopted by the government'.

Sousa Mendes also found it intolerable to be severely punished for acts which had prompted 'praise of the administration, both in Portugal and abroad'. There had surely been some mistake, he concluded, 'since those panegyrics should be addressed to the country and its population, whose altruistic and humanitarian feelings had universal repercussions'.

Since he received no reply, Sousa Mendes wrote to the

president of the republic on 24 February 1946, asking him to intervene: 'The constitution of the republic is not fascist, nor is the National Assembly fascist. Its deputies, if they wish to respect the constitution, cannot withhold justice from the man who obeyed the same constitution.'

Sousa Mendes never got any response. The stone that Salazar had placed on his dossier was still in place.

In March 1947, César, who was now the Portuguese ambassador to Switzerland, wrote another letter, this time to the Foreign Minister, whom he believed capable of getting the verdict on his brother reviewed. He once again drew attention to the physical, psychological and financial ills affecting Aristides, 'who owns nothing and is crippled with debt'. 'His children, who were studying at Bordeaux University, were forced to break off their studies without being able to stay in Portugal, and two of them, who were born in the United States, had to opt for American nationality, which meant they saw active service, from which, thank God, they returned safe and sound.

'My brother's sole motive in all his actions was to do good, and he cannot be allowed to die with an accusation that is as insulting as it is unjust hanging over him,' César concluded. 'We inherited an unblemished name from our parents, and we hope to pass it on in the same state to our children.' Aristides and César had clearly failed to understand that Salazar would never issue a 'pardon'.

★

In 1948, César's sons, José and Manuel, who were boarders at Lisbon's Academic College, visited their uncle and aunt in their little flat in Avenida de Berna. 'It was very sad,' José remembers. 'We were deeply shocked to see them in such a state. They were both very ill. "Tata Gigi" [Auntie Angelina] was in great pain. Their utterly devoted son, Luís Filipe, helped them as best he could. They were short of everything, even milk for breakfast. And yet Aristides joked and asked questions about our studies as though nothing was wrong. When we came out, I looked at Manuel, and he burst into tears.'

On 16 August 1948, Angelina, mother of fourteen, died of a stroke in Lisbon. She departed this world discreetly, seeking no plaudits for what she had done during her life, which she regarded as no more than her God-allotted destiny. In *O Cônsul*,[6] a novel she devoted to the life of Aristides de Sousa Mendes, Júlia Nery asks the following question: 'Had she not possessed the feelings of fraternity that are so characteristic of country people, which were never spoilt in her case by the petty-mindedness of the circles she moved in, would this mother of so many children have had the courage to support the consul?'

As she lay dying, Angelina had only one regret: that she was not surrounded by all her children. Manuel, possibly the brightest of them all, had died in Louvain; and the infant Raquel had been carried off at about the same time.

She thought of their big house in Louvain, where the

whole family used to live together. And she remembered Bordeaux, that frenzied period of her life when she had perhaps never been at once so close to and so distant from Aristides, and which had been destined by God as a penitence, redemption or blessing, but which they now had to struggle to pay for uncomplainingly.

She thought of her children. Where were they? Pedro Nuno, like Jules and Isabel, was in the Belgian Congo. Geraldo and Clotilde were in Angola, and Sebastião, Carlos, Teresinha, Joana and José in the United States.

Only three of her children were living in Portugal: Aristides was working in Viseu, and Luis Filipe and João Paulo in Lisbon – though not for much longer, since they both would shortly leave for Canada and the United States respectively.

As Nery writes:

For a long time [she] had been suspended in time by a kind of coma, behind a screen that separated her from real life. Since she had reigned over her household and had little contact with the spitefulness of the outside world, since she had not learnt to unravel the nest of thorns put in her way by polite society or swallow the broken glass of political intrigue, her mind had given way and her body failed to hold out for as long as her husband's. For she could no longer find any reason to hope for a return to better days.

Had it not been for Bordeaux, the folly of the human race, the din of battle, the barbarity of some, the cowardice of others and the heroism of a few, Aristides, Angelina and their children would have all been living at Passal, their mansion in Cabanas de Viriato, and Angelina could have died with the straightforward satisfaction of having conducted her life as she should.

Of what and of whom did Angelina de Sousa Mendes do Amaral e Abranches, a descendant of King João VI's private secretary, think as she breathed her last?

8. The Death of a Just Man

'Despite the fact that I have rather forgotten the things of this life, I have not yet got to the point where I have lost interest in everything, because of the number of people, children and grandchildren whom I love, and who also think of me.' Aristides wrote those rather disillusioned words on 26 July 1950, in the course of returning birthday greetings he had received from his twin brother, César. He had not however lost all hope that his situation might improve, since he asked César 'to try to find out what was happening as regards the amnesty'.

A few days later, in another letter to César, he thanked him for looking into the matter and told him he was going to write to the King of Belgium, who, he hoped, 'will take an interest in someone who has rendered such real services to the Belgians, without receiving anything in return'.

That same year, in another letter to César, Aristides wrote: 'Pedro Nuno, Maria Adelaide and their children are in financial straits. My salary has been used up paying for their outgoings, and that is why I'm asking you if you could help them. I've written to Sal [Salazar], who replied indirectly that he had passed my letter on to C.M. [Caeiro da Maia, the Foreign Minister].'

All these letters were sent by Aristides from Cabanas de Viriato. Since Angelina's death, he had been living there with Andrée Cibial, whom he married at San Juan church in Salamanca, Spain, on 16 October 1949.

That day, Andrée's childhood dream of marrying a consul came true – even though he was only a consul on half pay, lived alone in a house too big for him, and had been ostracized by many of his friends, even though, like some seasonal worker, he needed the permission of the authorities to be able to travel abroad, even though the days were well and truly over when he used to be posted to places with exotic names like San Francisco, Porto Alegre, Maranhão, Antwerp and Zanzibar.

No matter: she was the consul's wife, and she wanted to make him a gift of her love, her wild temperament and her fathomless devotion.

Aristides was a sick man. His right arm had been paralysed since his stroke in 1945. The couple divided their time between Cabanas de Viriato and Rua Filipe da Mata in Lisbon. 'Everything had changed,' Fernanda, the *'petiza'*, remembers.[1] 'You'd see him going for a walk, leaning on her, with his arm inside his overcoat. He still wanted to talk to everyone.' Fernanda feels that Aristides de Sousa Mendes's tragedy was 'more chilling, slower, more agonizing and more brutal than any car accident'.

On top of that, the authorities continued to pester him over petty administrative matters. Salazar needed only to lift a finger for Aristides de Sousa Mendes to be able to see out his final years in peace, but he still refused to pardon him. He bore the consul an undying grudge.

When Aristides asked Monsignor Manuel Gonçalves Cerejeira, the cardinal patriarch of Lisbon and one of the dictator's few close friends, to intercede with Salazar on his behalf, he replied: 'It would be a better idea for you to pray to Our Lady of Fátima.'

One is put in mind of La Fontaine's fable 'The Rat in the Hermitage'.

> 'A poor recluse, what power have I
> To succour your necessity
> Save to commend you to the grace divine?
> You have my prayers – I can no more.'
> And with these Words he slammed the door.[2]

As for Salazar's attitude to Sousa Mendes, it recalls the following passage in Julien Benda's *The Betrayal of the Intellectuals*:[3]

Tolstoy relates that when he was in the Army he saw one of his brother officers strike a man who fell out from the ranks during a march. Tolstoy said to him: 'Are you not ashamed to treat a fellow human being in this way? Have you not read the Gospels?'

The other officer replied: 'And have you not read Army Orders?'

Ministry of the Interior officials still loomed large in Sousa Mendes's life: he had to ask them for permission to go and get married to Andrée in Spain, and to bring her back to Portugal with him. At the beginning of the fifties, at a time when the developed world was about to experience one of its most spectacular economic and social revolutions, Portugal was a backwater shielded from progress by a moralistic dictator who was allergic to moral standards and preferred Machiavelli to St Paul.

The presidential election of 1949, the year that Portugal joined NATO, was little more than a sham. The opposition candidate, General Norton de Matos, withdrew before the opening of the poll to protest against its irregularity. The official candidate, Marshal Oscar Carmona, was 'elected'.

While Jacques Marcadé and some other historians believe that 'Salazarism had died in the fifties' and point to all the signs, however slight, that cracks in the edifice were beginning to appear during that decade, the dictator still kept Portugal in an iron grip, cracking down ever harder and exiling most of his opponents.

Salazar became an increasingly solitary figure whose

knowledge of the outside world was restricted to little more than a muffled echo by his protective collaborators. 'He had lost all contact with the younger generation,' says Adriano Moreira, who served under Salazar as Minister of Colonies. 'I remember having a conversation with him on the subject of racism; when I mentioned Frantz Fanon's novel, *Les Damnés de la terre*, he replied, to my amazement: "I haven't opened a novel in twenty years."'

Salazar never agreed to make a gesture in favour of Aristides de Sousa Mendes.

Accounts of Sousa Mendes's final years vary greatly. But all those who knew him at the time seem to agree on one thing: even when he was going through the hardest times, when he felt most rejected and humiliated, 'the consul' always looked on the bright side of life.

'I saw my uncle again at Mangualde,' says Aristides's nephew José. 'He seemed at peace with himself, and poked gentle fun at Andrée. He seemed to have a detached attitude to the world, as though he were somehow unconcerned by it.'

At Cabanas de Viriato, he wore the same clothes as before, and as stylishly as ever, though they were by now a little threadbare. And he still liked to sport his 'diplomat's hat'.

Sousa Mendes had always had financial problems, but now they were getting steadily worse. He never had any money sense, and Andrée even less so than he. They were similar in other respects too, for instance in their love of music. Andrée was not a stay-at-home sort of person – 'Indeed she never had a home,' says Marie-Rose, her daughter by Sousa Mendes, with gentle irony. 'Yet she often spoke to me about the wonderful big house that the three of us would one day live in.'

Although Sousa Mendes and Andrée were destitute, there was quite a jolly atmosphere at Cabanas. One evening, for example, they were expecting friends – the few they still had – for dinner. Everyone had arrived. But Andrée, whose idea of punctuality was as vague as her notion of thrift, and who hated anything she saw as an obligation, was nowhere to be seen. In fact she was upstairs in her room. Realizing she did not have a single dress she wanted to wear, she took down a red velvet curtain, swathed herself in it and descended the stairs to join her guests. 'She was ravishing,' Sousa Mendes later told Marie-Rose.

José Fidalgo, who worked as their chauffeur at Cabanas, came almost every day to pick up Aristides and Andrée and take them to Viseu or some other destination. 'One day they couldn't stop giggling during the drive,' he remembers. 'She said she was pregnant. I can still hear the car ringing with her laughter.' A few weeks later, Andrée had a miscarriage.

Sousa Mendes would still occasionally go for walks in the village, but they became shorter and shorter. He would stop for a long time at the chemist's and have lengthy chats with its owner, José Borges Dinis.

The people of Cabanas did not much take to Andrée, 'the foreigner', or 'the Frenchwoman', whom they held responsible for the family's misfortunes. They also criticized her for having 'ruined' Sousa Mendes and gradually sold off all the furniture in the family mansion, Passal.

It is true that the house was gradually emptying. But it was hardly Andrée's fault. Sousa Mendes was up to his ears in debt and could no longer make ends meet. The banks were breathing harder and harder down his neck. An antique dealer from Oporto came to buy one of the pianos, then the other. 'In more prosperous times, everyone used to sponge on him, and, as the saying goes, he who gives away his fortune ends up a beggar,' says one of the characters in Júlia Nery's novel *O Cônsul*.[4] One by one the bedrooms were emptied of their furniture.

Marie-Rose lived in Ribérac with her uncle and aunt. Her mother would go to see her from time to time – always without warning, and always broke. She sometimes even turned up without her luggage, having had to leave it at a hotel because she could not pay the bill. Marie-Rose had been told that her father was a Portuguese diplomat who had been punished because he had disobeyed his government. No one mentioned all the people he had saved in Bordeaux. She was given a protected upbringing by her uncle and aunt, far from her not very maternal mother and legendary father.

Marie-Rose met Sousa Mendes for the first time in 1951, when she made her first Holy Communion: 'It was such a lovely surprise! He spoke very good French, with just a hint of a Portuguese accent. He was kind and attentive, and looked at the homework I'd done.'

Sousa Mendes returned to Ribérac on two other occasions. He seemed to find the town and its calm atmosphere very congenial. 'He gave me a gramophone, and I remember him laughing and humming the tune of a song of the period – Maria Cândido's "*J'Attendrai*", I think.'

Sousa Mendes loved to take his daughter to school and meet her girlfriends. And he would also come to fetch her in the afternoon, even though it was quite a long walk and he had increasing difficulty in getting around. 'He always talked about the present, never about what he'd done in Portugal,' says Marie-Rose. 'He always wore dark clothes, and at the beginning of each afternoon he would take a rosary out of his pocket and spend some considerable time in prayer.'

At the beginning of 1952, Aristides and Andrée asked Marie-Rose, who was then twelve, if she would like to go and live with them in Portugal. 'I said no, because my life was here with my aunt and uncle, who had brought me up. But I cried a great deal,' she explains. Her decision was understandable. How could she leave her home to go and live with a mother who was always rubbing people up the wrong way? 'My father was more affectionate than my mother,' Marie-Rose admits. But she also talks about her eccentric mother with admirable restraint and, in the last account, great affection: 'She had such a fertile imagination that she didn't need books when, on evenings when she was here, she wanted to tell me stories of astronauts who lived on the moon.' Although Andrée never told Marie-Rose about what had happened in Bordeaux, she repeatedly said that her father had been unfairly punished by Salazar and that she would manage to prove it. Right up until her death, Andrée ruined herself paying lawyers' fees in an attempt to obtain compensation.

At the end of 1952 Sousa Mendes had another stroke and had to have an operation. Life then became increasingly difficult. He and Andrée lived in one of the first-floor bed-rooms, with the shutters almost always closed. From time to time, a villager did a little housework for them. The barber, José Fernandes de Campos Melo, came to shave him three times a week.

'The house was just as imposing as it had always been,' he remembers. 'But it got emptier and emptier. The consul was as nice as ever, and sometimes even cracked jokes though he was increasingly handicapped.'

After selling the antique furniture, the pianos, the big tables and the bookcases, the couple had to say goodbye to beds, armchairs and chairs. Then it came to the point where they were forced to sell baths, sinks, pipes and curtain rails for next to nothing.

Geraldo's son, António, remembers a very painful scene: 'I was very small. I came with my mother to Cabanas to see my grandfather and take him a box of cakes. We knocked on the door, but there was no answer. Then we knocked harder and harder. My mother wanted to go and call the police. After a time, I saw the shadowy figure of a man with completely white hair standing at a first-floor window and looking down at us. My mother showed him the cakes. A few minutes later, the front door half-opened and a hand – just a hand – slipped out and took the box of cakes. Then the door closed. And that was all.'

A document dated January 1953 shows that Andrée sold virtually the whole contents of the house for 15,000 escudos. The banks were bombarding them with final demands. Andrée and Aristides were forced to burn what remained in the house so as to keep warm. Fernanda later remembered: 'The consul nearly starved and froze to death as he tried to burn the doors of the house, when he no longer had the strength to throw the planks on to the fire.'[5]

As he was paralysed, Sousa Mendes found it increasingly difficult to write. Almost all his last letters were written by someone else – Andrée no doubt – and he could only just manage to sign them. 'I have high hopes of coming to visit you in Africa,' he 'wrote' to Pedro Nuno, then in the Congo, enclosing a photograph with the letter.

He tried to write, on his own, a letter to César. The writing is that of a five-year-old child and virtually illegible. It is possible to make out the words: 'I've spent the last few days with many sacrifices!'

Sousa Mendes insisted on travelling to Ribérac again. Marie-Rose, her uncle and her aunt came to fetch him in Périgueux at the end of February 1954. They took a taxi to Ribérac. 'His whole right side was paralysed,' Marie-Rose remembers. 'At table, he had difficulty in using his knife and fork. He had to guide his right arm with his left hand in order to pick up a knife. He used to fall asleep at table, and during the night he would fall out of bed. During the day he walked very slowly with a stick – his right leg was completely rigid.'

Sousa Mendes's state of health worsened each day. Andrée took him to see a doctor in Ribérac. Then they stayed for a time with Andrée's brother in Angoulême. At the end of March, Sousa Mendes decided to return to Lisbon. Even though his country had caused him such suffering, that was where he wanted to end his days.

He was taken to the Ordem Terceira de São Francisco Hospital in Lisbon, a large building in the Chiado district, which was run by the Third Order of Franciscans. Aristides, like César, had been very drawn to St Francis of Assisi and the order he founded. César, as can be seen from some of his letters, even thought of joining the order. It is possible that Aristides may have belonged to the Third Order of Franciscans in Louvain, though there is no firm evidence that this was so.

After suffering another stroke and pneumonia, Sousa Mendes died in mid-afternoon on 3 April 1954. The only person present when he died was one of his nieces, Madalena.

After his death his body was clothed in a Franciscan monk's habit.

Father Cuthbert's *La Vie de saint François d'Assise*[6] concludes as follows: 'He was not of this world, yet this world loved him and, in its clumsy way, revered him. It was the same when he died as it had been during his life; but, whereas the world acted clumsily, there were men, a large number of men, who loved Saint Francis's spirit and understood him. He had not lived in vain.'

Fernanda remarks sadly: 'He died where he was born – except that he was born in a palace and died destitute. It was as if Jesus Christ had been killed a second time.'[7]

The next day, his body was placed in a chapel of rest in the middle of São Sebastião da Pedreira church. There was almost no one to keep vigil over him. A member of the family sped to Mangualde to tell César that his twin brother had died. There were fears he would take it very badly.

The coffin then left by train for Cabanas de Viriato. At Oliveirinha station it was placed on a fire engine, which took it to the village church. The vehicle, a bright red Hudson Supersix, which had been donated to the town of Cabanas after the war by Sousa Mendes's Belgian friends, was a strange and marvellous symbol: painted on its bonnet were the words *Uma vida por uma vida* (A life for a life). The funeral mass was given in the church opposite Passal.

José wrote in his diary: 'God, please save uncle Aristides's soul.'

On 5 April, César de Sousa Mendes received a visiting card from the Portuguese prime minister, António de Oliveira Salazar. It bore just two words: 'My condolences.'

9. A Tree in Jerusalem

On 21 February 1961, a tree was planted in honour of Aristides de Sousa Mendes in the Garden of the Righteous in Jerusalem. On 13 March 1988, the Portuguese national assembly voted unanimously in favour of his rehabilitation – forty-eight years after the events in Bordeaux. Had it not been for his persistent, loving and close-knit family, and the efforts of a handful of loyal friends, the memory of the consul of Bordeaux might never have been honoured.

It was Pedro Nuno who set in motion the lengthy process that resulted in Sousa Mendes's rehabilitation. He was in the Congo when his father died. In the senior ranks of the Belgian administration of the colony, there was a man who had heard of the exploits of the Portuguese consul in Bordeaux. Pedro Nuno knew him, and together they made sure that a local newspaper, the *Pourquoi Pas?*, carried an obituary of Sousa Mendes.

So it was that at the end of April 1954, in a country very far from Bordeaux and Lisbon, the first tribute to the consul was published. Under the headline 'A Great Friend of Belgium Dies', the paper outlined the career of the former consul in Antwerp and described his actions in Bordeaux at the beginning of the war. It concluded: 'All those who knew him will be deeply affected by the death of such a generous man. His undying memory will remain engraved on their hearts for ever.'

It was not much of a tribute, just a few lines in a newspaper in a remote outpost, but enough to ensure that the flame was not snuffed out. Sebastião, the 'American', took over. In 1948, when his mother died, he had promised Aristides he 'would tell the whole world what he had done in Bordeaux in 1940'. Every evening, after his day's work at an American bank, he wrote *Flight through Hell*,[1] in which he related in the form of a short story – everyone realized it was fact, not fiction – his father's and his own experiences. When Aristides read the manuscript, he said: 'Everything you describe is correct.'

In May 1954, one month after his father's death, Sebastião wrote:

Today, presumably alive and happy, the refugees of long ago give little or no thought to those far-gone tragic days. [. . .] They did not know then and they do not know now that one man thought of them and saved them. Today, the man who sacrificed all he ever had is dead and buried – but not forgotten! He never regretted his action and he died a true Christian.

Was he a great man? Was he mad in showing so little instinct for self-preservation? The answer lies in all of us when we try to pass judgement on him. I know all that, and much more besides [. . .]. I was, or rather I am, his son. In any case I am proud of the fact that I was lucky enough to have such a man as my father.

Any father anywhere would have been delighted for his son to have written those lines.

Then it was Joana's turn to keep the flame alive. With the help of her sister Teresinha, she contacted a number of Jewish refugees in the United States who had been saved by her father. She also wrote to the Israeli prime minister, David Ben Gurion, to tell him about her father's heroic conduct during the war. The directors of the Yad Vashem Center in Jerusalem were asked to look into the matter.

The centre, which was set up in the fifties to keep alive memories of the Shoah, is both a study centre and a memorial. It is the body which, after thorough investigation, awards the title of Righteous among the Nations to any non-Jew who saved Jews during the war.

In 1961, just as they were beginning to lose hope, Joana and Teresinha received a letter from the Israeli authorities, informing them that a tree would be planted at the Yad Vashem Museum in Jerusalem in honour of Sousa Mendes. That was duly done on 21 February.

Several articles subsequently appeared in the American

press, notably in the *Reader's Digest* of March 1963, where George Kent mentioned Sousa Mendes in a list of people who had saved Jews during the war.

Harry Ezratty contributed an article entitled 'The Portuguese Consul and the 10,000 Jews' to the September–October 1964 issue of *Jewish Life*. He concluded:

> But those Jews who still live today because of his sacrifice are a tribute to his noble deeds. If each one remembers the man who gave him succour and lives a life inspired by Aristides de Sousa Mendes's principles, he will have accomplished even more than Mendes dreamed.

In 1967, Yad Vashem struck a commemorative medallion, reading 'To Aristides de Sousa Mendes, from the grateful Jewish people', which may be regarded as the highest tribute the association was accustomed to pay. On the back of the medallion was a Talmudic dictum: 'One who saves a human life saves as it were a whole world.' A ceremony was organized at the Israeli consulate in New York in the presence of Joana, Sebastião, João Paulo (who had by then become John Paul Abranches), Teresinha, Luís Filipe and Rabbi Kruger.

All the North American-based members of the family – Sebastião, John Paul, Joana, Teresinha and José – continued the campaign in the United States and Canada. They were no longer alone. They gathered as many eye-witness accounts as they could from both ordinary people and eminent figures like Otto of Habsburg, the Grand Duchess of Luxembourg and Professor Charles Oulmont.

They were naturally helped by Rabbi Kruger's daughter and son. The children of Sousa Mendes and Kruger worked together just as their fathers had done thirty years before. They were also assisted by an American senator of Portuguese descent, Tony Coelho.

In June 1986, John Paul organized a petition for the rehabilitation of Sousa Mendes which was signed by 2,800 people, published in *The New York Times*, and sent to the Portuguese government. In 1987, again at the initiative of Tony Coelho, the US House of Representatives adopted the following resolution: 'Paying special tribute to Dr de Sousa Mendes for his extraordinary acts of mercy and justice during World War II.' Representative Robert Jacobvitz received a letter from none other than Ted Kennedy, who told him that he was the 'co-sponsor' of the resolution, and that he was at his disposal for any other action in Sousa Mendes's favour.

As for Otto of Habsburg, in a letter dated 16 September 1986, he wrote to António, Sousa Mendes's grandson: 'I would like to tell you once more in writing how eternally grateful I am to your grandfather. He was a great gentleman, a man of admirable courage and integrity who obeyed his principles at the expense of his personal interest. At a time when many were cowards, he was a veritable hero of the West; you can be proud of your grandfather.'

Also in 1986, an American delegation that included Coelho went to Lisbon to sign a trade agreement between the United States and Portugal. It is easy to imagine the amazement of the Portuguese officials when their American opposite numbers, at a point when they were not discussing purely technical matters, insisted that Sousa Mendes be honoured in his own country.

And that is how, strangely, the first official ceremony concerning the rehabilitation of Aristides de Sousa Mendes by his country's government took place on 24 May 1987, at the Portuguese embassy in Washington. On that occasion, Mário Soares, who was then president of the republic, post-humously decorated Sousa Mendes with the Order of Liberty.

But it was not until 13 March 1988 that the Lisbon parliament officially rehabilitated Aristides de Sousa Mendes – forty-eight years after his great Bordeaux rescue operation, but also fourteen years after the overthrow of the dictatorship.

It is difficult to explain why the new regime, which came to power as a result of the 'Carnation Revolution' of April 1974, was so slow in acting. Those who brought down the dictatorship were in many cases too young to have experienced the war years. Others, with greater political experience like Álvaro Cunhal and Soares, had not known Sousa Mendes, who never formed part of the political opposition to the Salazar regime. In their eyes, he remained a monarchist aristocrat who had never been sent to jail or exiled.

As a result, Soares, who was Foreign Minister in the first democratic government in 1974, did not reply to the letters that Joana sent him. His successor, Captain Melo Antunes, was more responsive to the cause: in May 1976 he asked Dr Nuno Álvares Adrião de Bessa Lopes, a fifty-nine-year-old diplomat whose career had been destroyed by the Salazar regime, to look into the case of Sousa Mendes.

The first thing Bessa Lopes did was to locate and open up the Sousa Mendes file that had been sealed and put away in the strongroom of the Foreign Ministry archives. In other words, he raised the stone that Salazar had placed on the case for all eternity.

His daughter, Isabel Ferreiro, remembers: 'He spent two weeks working almost night and day on the hundreds of pages in the dossier. Then he said to me: "We must rehabilitate the memory of a hero who had the courage to do what he did at the risk of ruining his career and the lives of the members of his family."'

Bessa Lopes wrote a long report, confirming first of all that there was a law which would permit the 'posthumous and immediate reinstatement' of Sousa Mendes and that all the documents pleaded in favour of his rehabilitation. 'Aristides de Sousa Mendes did not shout from the rooftops, nor did he exploit or embroider the services he rendered. His family had at first hoped that the rout of fascism in Europe would enable Sousa Mendes to be rehabilitated, and then also believed it would happen with the demise of fascism in Portugal.'

Bessa Lopes also waxed indignant about documents in the file which tried to prove that the Mendes family was descended from Jews who were converted to Christianity in 1497. 'Sousa Mendes,' Bessa Lopes wrote, 'had been unable to escape from the clutches of the new inquisitors, who are skilled at destroying people mentally, at mounting conspiracies, at sullying consciences and reputations, and at manipulating public opinion.'

By way of conclusion, Bessa Lopes wrote: 'Aristides de Sousa Mendes was condemned for having refused to be an accomplice to Nazi war crimes. That was the sense and human significance of his disobedience.'

Bessa Lopes did not personally see his efforts rewarded, since he died in 1982. According to his daughter, he repeated only a fortnight before his death that Sousa Mendes was a hero who thoroughly deserved to be rehabilitated.

But there was another element in the equation: the cowardice and conformism of the civil service. In 1977, the secretary general of the Foreign Ministry ruled that it was not an opportune time to rehabilitate Sousa Mendes. The drift of his argument was that it would mean rehabilitating someone who had disobeyed and thus discredit all those who had obeyed. So it was not until 13 March 1988 that the Chamber of Deputies voted unanimously in favour of Sousa Mendes's rehabilitation.

There have been many other tokens of gratitude elsewhere in the world. The name of Sousa Mendes has been given to a forest of 10,000 trees in the Negev desert and to a square in Tel Aviv. In Portugal there are now eight streets and a secondary school in Póvoa de Santa Iria, in the suburbs of Lisbon, that are named after the consul. The idea was even mooted at one point of calling the new bridge over the Tagus in Lisbon after Sousa Mendes. In Montreal a plaque in a children's playground explains his story.

It took more than fifty years for the city of Bordeaux to pay tribute to Aristides de Sousa Mendes. That it did so at all was the result of a tireless campaign by an outstanding man, Father Jacques Rivière, a Capuchin monk and worker-priest also known as Brother Bernard. A wiry man who always goes around with a sailor's cap rammed on to his head, he has devoted part of his life to the Portuguese immigrant community in Bordeaux. He worked as a house painter, as well as hosting a programme on La Clef des Ondes, a local radio station, aimed at Bordeaux's large Portuguese community.

He discovered the story of Sousa Mendes in 1987 when listening to a Portuguese radio station. He was both extremely moved and fascinated by it, and failed to understand why no one in Bordeaux had ever referred to it, or why there was no trace of Sousa Mendes's exploits in the city's Musée Jean-Moulin, which is supposed to be a shrine in memory of the Resistance.

Along with a few friends, including Manuel Dias, the

prefect's adviser on immigration, Rivière tirelessly moved heaven and earth to get Bordeaux, in turn, to pay tribute to Aristides de Sousa Mendes. He knew that breaking down the resistance of those who preferred to cast a discreet veil over the events of 1940 would be an uphill task. Even the leaders of the Jewish community did not seem all that keen on the idea. Neither did the then Portuguese consul.

In September 1987 Rivière wrote an article about Sousa Mendes in *Interaction Aquitaine Portugal*, a newsletter published by him which caters to the Portuguese community in south-west France. His article had an unexpectedly moving outcome: it was by reading it that Marie-Rose, the daughter of Aristides de Sousa Mendes and Andrée Cibial who was then living in Pau, discovered the truth about her father.

'I had already read a few lines about my father in the *Reader's Digest* in 1963,' says Marie-Rose. 'At the time I asked the Portuguese consulate in Bayonne if they had any further information about him. They didn't. It was when I read the issue of *Interaction Aquitaine Portugal* devoted to Aristides de Sousa Mendes that I discovered the whole story.'

Marie-Rose contacted Rivière, and, along with Dias, they set up the National Committee in Homage to Aristides de Sousa Mendes, of which she became the president. In June 1990, for the fiftieth anniversary of June 1940, the International Committee for the Commemoration of Dr Aristides de Sousa Mendes, whose president is John Paul Abranches, arrived in Bordeaux, and Marie-Rose met for the first time some of her half-brothers and half-sisters, who embraced her warmly.

The filming, partly in Bordeaux, of Diana Andringa's *O Cônsul Injustiçado* (*The Proscribed Consul*), a co-production between Portuguese television and France 3 Aquitaine which was directed by Teresa Olga, eventually brought home the exemplary nature of Sousa Mendes's conduct even to those who were least keen on a commemoration. This was chiefly due to the fact that many of the refugees who had been in Bordeaux in 1940 were prepared to come from very far away to describe their experiences in front of the Portuguese journalist's camera.

It was on 29 May 1994 that Bordeaux finally paid Aristides de Sousa Mendes the tribute he deserved. Present at the ceremony were Mário Soares, then Portuguese president, and his wife, Maria Barroso, as well as the prefect of the Gironde department, Landouzy, the co-president of B'nai Brith in Bordeaux, Claudine Geissmann, the president of the consistory, Dr Alexis Banayan, a deputy mayor, Dmitri Lavroff, and the Portuguese and Israeli ambassadors.

First of all, Soares unveiled a bust of Aristides de Sousa Mendes on Esplanade Charles-de-Gaulle and laid a spray of flowers at the foot of the monument. Then a plaque was unveiled on the wall of Quai Louis-XVIII. 'Aristides de Sousa Mendes applied the biblical principle that a man has the right to refuse an order which is unethical,' Dr Banayan declared.

Then Soares spoke: 'It is a great honour and a very moving moment for me to be here to pay tribute to Aristides de Sousa Mendes, a great Portuguese figure, a simple and modest man who managed to perform his duties as a human being against the orders of the dictator Salazar.'

A new edition of Jocelyn Gille's strip cartoon, *Bordeaux dans la tourmente* (*Bordeaux in Turmoil*),[2] containing several pages devoted to Sousa Mendes, was also presented on that occasion.

In the following day's issue of the daily *Sud-Ouest*, Bertrand Poupard wrote:

For some years now, international law and the political discourse have talked about a new notion in the relationship between countries, which is called 'the right to intervene'. Yesterday morning in Bordeaux, Mário Soares and his Bordelais hosts [. . .] frequently insisted, in one way or another, in asides or in speeches, on the importance of another duty of mankind: the duty to disobey one's government, which, if it could effectively operate in countries that are now the scene of ethnic cleansing, tribal massacres and social exclusion according to racial origin, would probably have meant we would not have needed to invent the right to intervene.

Rivière and his friends have not given up their campaign: they would like a Rue Sousa-Mendes to be officially inaugurated in Bordeaux and a school in the region named after the consul.

In October 1996, the Teatro de Portalegre troupe put on a play in Bordeaux, *Aristides, o Cônsul Que Desobedeceu* (*Aristides, the Consul Who Disobeyed*), written by Aristides's grandson, António de Moncada de Sousa Mendes.

The Sousa Mendes family would also like some sort of tribute to be paid to Angelina, Aristides's self-effacing wife. In a memorandum he sent to Yad Vashem in 1998, Pedro Nuno wrote: 'It is our duty to pay tribute to our mother [. . .]. I realize that tributes to our father never made any mention of her [. . .]. When my parents and I were in Bordeaux in 1940, the doors of our home were opened to many refugees, some elderly, some less so, most of whom were Jews.

'They settled on to our sofas and armchairs. Some even lay on the carpet. I remember that period very well and I have had many contacts with those refugees. From that moment on, our mother looked after not only her children but also the refugees, who worried her, irrespective of their origins; they experienced the generosity and altruism of our mother, who was already fifty-two years old. In many cases, she assisted them with great affection, and gave them food and drink. When others came into the kitchen where we took our meals, she served them without ever complaining.

'Even on the most difficult days, she never held anything against our father and always stood by his side. She never opposed what our father was doing to save the refugees, nor did any of his children ever criticize him. She was a good wife, a good mother, a good Christian, and we thank God for that.'

The Sousa Mendes family would also like to receive proper financial compensation from the Portuguese state, which it would use to set up a foundation and, possibly, convert Passal into a museum. Aníbal Cavaco Silva's stingy conservative government got the civil service to calculate the compensation. Working on the basis of 1940 currency values, it came up with the figure of 750,000 escudos, or about the equivalent of £2,500, as compensation for the shattered lives of a husband, a wife and fourteen children.

The Socialists turned out to be slightly more generous: they offered 15 million escudos, or the equivalent of about £50,000. But it was still far below what the Sousa Mendes family were holding out for. 'We're not beggars,' says António, one of the grandsons, 'but after what the Portuguese state did to my grandfather we're not asking for charity, but simply justice.'

But they have not yet won their case. In the Palácio das Necessidades, which still houses the Foreign Ministry, there remain many who condemn Sousa Mendes's disobedience. 'He is still often a taboo subject,' says Bessa Lopes's daughter.

Calvet de Magalhães, for example, who joined the ministry in 1941 and was a very close friend of Salazar's, feels Sousa Mendes is rather a sensitive subject. While he sympathizes with him, he also describes his attitude as 'rather extravagant for a diplomat' and says he was 'never taken very seriously in the ministry'.

Adriano Moreira, who began his career in 1946, and who served as a minister in Salazar's government before becoming a university professor, has a completely opposite opinion. In his view, 'Aristides de Sousa Mendes's action marks a turning point in the history of international law. From our Western perspective, the legitimacy of political power, which is based on the will of the people, is an original legitimacy; I have been elected democratically, therefore I am legitimate. That legitimacy is no longer adequate. We now need a legitimacy of practice: what have I done with that power? Aristides de Sousa Mendes attacked a principle which had hitherto been absolute: the original legitimacy must be obeyed. The Nuremberg tribunal established that people are also responsible to certain principles and that they cannot act against human values. The great quality of Sousa Mendes was that he obeyed the values of mankind.'

The metro station Parque, in Lisbon's business quarter, is devoted to human rights. Aristides de Sousa Mendes has a place of honour in it. In the vast entrance hall, a spotlight focuses on a tiny medal bearing the effigy of the consul which is embedded in a block of concrete. The visual contrast is designed to evoke the loneliness of a man at the precise moment when he had to take the most momentous decision in his life: whether or not to obey inhuman orders.

On the walls alongside the escalators that take passengers down to the platforms there are quotations from writers, philosophers and poets from all over the world. One of them is a line by the Portuguese poet, Fernando Pessoa: 'I have a headache and a worldache.'

Epilogue

Passal, where the spirit of Aristides de Sousa Mendes lives on

With his white hair, dark overcoat and discreetly noble bearing, the elderly man who came to meet me at Sintra station stood out from the crowd of people waiting for the arrival of the Lisbon train. Pedro Nuno de Sousa Mendes was then seventy-eight, and the oldest of Aristides's surviving children. After his exile in the Congo, then in Belgium, he returned home. The child in scout's uniform who smiled at the camera in front of their house in Louvain, the unruly teenager who designed the Expresso dos Montes Hermínios coach, the diligent student who gave his father constant physical and moral support in Bordeaux, the devoted husband of Maria Adelaide, who was always at his side, had suffered a great deal. Yet he was serene.

I listened to him as he described his story and that of his father in French, which he spoke with a soft, almost lisping

Portuguese accent. After seeing his eyes successively sparkle or mist over with tears as certain memories flooded back, after being struck by the immense generosity of all his remarks – he had not a bad word to say of anyone – it seems almost out of place for me to add anything more.

Yet the story of Sousa Mendes needs to be concluded. César did not long survive his twin brother. He died at his house in Mangualde on 18 July 1955. A few weeks earlier, his son José, realizing that his father did not have long to live, sent him a letter which he describes today as 'an expression of very profound and very deeply-felt filial love'. It contained the following sentence: 'I cannot forget your twin brother, who was such a pleasant and good man, and who suffered much because he loved much.'

Andrée Cibial died in Pau in 1991, after squandering the little money she still had on lawyers' fees in an attempt to enforce the claims she imagined she had to the lost estates in Cabanas de Viriato. From time to time she would be spotted in the village, clutching a sheaf of papers. 'After my father's death, she went off, came back and went off again. She spent her whole life doing that,' her daughter Marie-Rose explains. Andrée's final years were an ordeal. At one point, she spent almost a year in a Paris squat without either water or electricity. After suffering a heart attack, she was treated in Périgueux, not far from where her daughter and son-in-law lived. She was then transferred to an old people's home in Pau, where she died, with her daughter at her side.

Fernanda, the '*petiza*', is now seventy-eight and lives in Oporto. She is caught between a desire to forget the painful episodes in her life and her hero-worship of Aristides de Sousa Mendes, 'the most just man and the saint who suffered most in the whole history of the world', as she puts it.

On 27 July 1970, Salazar died. After suffering a stroke on 17 September 1968, he was replaced as prime minister by Marcelo Caetano, a former rector of Lisbon University. Initially, by implementing measures that were mere window-dressing, Caetano tried to 'liberalize' a regime that was foundering. He subsequently reverted to more traditional repressive methods. In 1969 there were violent demonstrations at Coimbra University. Industrial action spread like wildfire, Portugal's colonial wars were becoming increasingly unpopular, and the political opposition had begun to organize itself. Even some leading members of the regime's main sources of support, the army and the church, started to distance themselves from it.

Salazar's death took place in an atmosphere of considerable indifference. Paul-Jean Franceschini, in an article that appeared in the French daily *Le Monde* on 28 July 1970, wrote:

The elderly fine-featured, white-haired gentleman from Lisbon, whose manners could be both courteous and brusque, and who cultivated an old-fashioned elegance with his severe suits and ankle-boots, dis-

concerted people much more than he made them indignant or won them over. [. . .] His admirers – mostly
people who worshipped the principle of authority –
tried to turn a frosty, starchy armchair dictator into a
human being, but with little success.

Miguel Torga[1] was responsible for the fairest, but also the
most damning, verdict on the dictator:

Salazar is dead. Too late for him, and also for those of
us who fought him. Too late for him because he did
not die in a blaze of glory as he must always have hoped;
and too late for us, who did not see him die at the
height of our fury, our humiliation and our revolt.

He lived an emotionless life, consciously, hiding
beneath a cloche of icy sternness, and inspiring fear
in others; and he died an emotionless death, uncon-
sciously, gently slipping away, and no longer inspiring
anything but pity.

So when we learnt a short while ago that he had at
last died, not the slightest quiver of emotion could be
sensed among either his supporters or his enemies.

Whereas the memory of the dictator has faded away and
is now reduced to a few lines in the history books, the
memory of the man he hounded so vindictively is now
honoured throughout the world.

Notes

Chapter 1: The Twins of Beira Alta

1. Fernando Dacosta, author of *Máscaras de Salazar* (Editorial Notícias, 1997) and other works.
2. Hélène Gourby, in *Le Portugal*, Larousse, 1989.
3. Jean-François Labourdette, *Histoire du Portugal*, 'Que Sais-je?', Presses Universitaires Françaises, 1995.
4. Jacques Marcadé, *Le Portugal au XXe siècle*, Presses Universitaires Françaises, 1988.
5. Paul-Jean Franceschini, *Le Monde*, 28 July 1970.
6. Labourdette, *Histoire*.
7. ibid.
8. ibid.

Chapter 2: The Carefree Happiness of a Large Family

1. Veríssimo Serrão, *História de Portugal*, Edições Verbo, 1990.
2. Jacques Marcadé, *Le Portugal au XXe siècle*.
3. António Ferro, *Salazar, le Portugal et son chef*, Grasset, 1934, a French translation of his *O Homem e a Sua Obra*, Edições do Templo, undated.
4. Mário Soares, *Le Portugal bâillonné: témoignage*, Paris, Calmann-Lévy, 1972.
5. Preface to *Lisbonne*, by Fernando Pessoa, 10/18, Editions Anatolia, 1995.
6. *Colóquio*, N°. 100, November–December 1987.

Chapter 3: Why Does a Man Start Disobeying?

1. 'Memórias de uma empregada' ('The Souvenirs of a Housemaid'), *Expresso*, 9 November 1996.
2. Miguel Torga, *La Création du Monde*, Aubier, 1982.
3. Jean Chédaille, *Bordeaux, capitale de la France*, Editions CMD, 1998.
4. Dominique Lormier, *Bordeaux pendant l'Occupation*, Editions Sud-Ouest, 1992.
5. Chédaille, *Bordeaux*.

Chapter 4: *'From now on, there will be no more nationalities, races or religions'*

1. Michael d'Avranches, *Flight through Hell*, Fédération des Associations Franco-Portugaises, 1951.
2. Chédaille, *Bordeaux*.
3. Jean Sévilla, *Zita, Impératrice Courage*, Perrin, 1997.
4. Chédaille, *Bordeaux*.

Chapter 5: *'I'll save you all!'*

1. D'Avranches, *Flight through Hell*.
2. Rui Afonso, *Um Homem Bom, Aristides de Sousa Mendes, o 'Wallenberg portugês'*, Caminho, 1995.
3. ibid.
4. Chédaille, *Bordeaux*.

Chapter 6: *The Revenge of the Nonentities*

1. Douglas Wheeler, 'And Who Is My Neighbor? A World War II Hero of Conscience for Portugal', *Luso-Brazilian Review XXVI*, University of Wisconsin Press, 1989.
2. Mariana Tavares Dias, *Lisboa nos Anos 40*, Quimera, 1997.

3. Yves Léonard, *Salazarisme et fascisme*, preface by Mário Soares, Editions Chandeigne, 1996.
4. Pedro Teotónio Pereira, *Memórias*, Edições Verbo, 1973.

Chapter 7: 'We are all refugees'

1. 'Memórias de uma empregada'.
2. Léonard, *Salazarisme et fascisme*.
3. Joseph Goebbels, *The Goebbels Diaries*, translated and edited by Louis P. Lockner, Hamish Hamilton, London, 1948.
4. Soares, *Le Portugal bâillonné*.
5. D'Avranches, *Flight through Hell*.
6. Júlia Nery, *O Cônsul*, Publicações Dom Quixote, Lisbon, 1991 (French translation by Claire Cayron: *La Résolution de Bordeaux*, Editions Le Mascaret, Bordeaux, 1993).

Chapter 8: The Death of a Just Man

1. 'Memórias de uma empregada'.
2. La Fontaine, *Fables* (Fable No. 3, Book 7), translated by Sir Edward Marsh, Dent, 1966.
3. Julien Benda, *The Betrayal of the Intellectuals*, translated by Richard Aldington, The Beacon Press, 1955.
4. Nery, *O Cônsul*.

5. 'Memórias de uma empregada'.
6. Father Cuthbert, *La Vie de saint François d'Assise*, Duculot, Gembloux, 1927.
7. 'Memórias de uma empregada'.

Chapter 9: *A Tree in Jerusalem*

1. D'Avranches, *Flight through Hell*.
2. Jocelyn Gille, *Bordeaux dans la tourmente*, J. Gille Editeur, 1994.

Epilogue

1. Miguel Torga, *En franchise intérieure, journal 1933–1977*, Aubier, 1982.

Index

— d.º —	65
— d.º —	65
— d.º —	65
— d.º —	65
em passaporte de Maddelini Steen	128
— d.º — Emilie Steen	12
do de ins. Felix Alberto Rodrigues	1
aporte — d.º —	9
passaporte Marco Marcus	12
Searce Mc Daniel	12
Antoni Slonimski	1
Janina Slonimska	12
Eruwim Slonimska	12
Eruwim Juljam	1
Viktor Fischer	1
Alice Fischer	1
Malvina Fgrb	1
Adelaide Wolstenholm	1
Louise Gabriel	1
Barbara de Garcia	1
Ian Carlos de Garcia	1
Ethel May Smith	1
Robert Montgomery	1
Bruno Dionizio	1
Lilly Natathion	
Masterowr Camille	
Master Leo	
Master Julius	
Blicky Eduard	
Blicky marie Lo